How To Quit Your Job
With
Passive Income

*Ultimate Beginners Guide
to* **Wealth and Riches** *with
12 Proven Businesses
You Can Start Today*

DUSTIN HEINER

*"What's the point of being alive if you don't at least
try to do something remarkable." - Anonymous*

Master Passive Income

www.masterpassiveincome.com

Copyright © 2016 Dustin Matsuhashi Heiner

Published by Triune Publications

Printed in the United States of America

ISBN-10: 0-9975155-5-4

ISBN-13: 978-0-9975155-5-8

To my lovely bride Melissa and my amazing children Ellie, Elias, Xander, and Faith Without you, none of this would matter. Thank you for being my inspiration and motivation.

To the Lord Jesus Christ who makes all things possible and who loves me and gave Himself up for me.

CONTENTS

READ THIS FIRST!

Free Cheat Sheet for this book!

DOWNLOAD THE CHEAT SHEET NOW!

"HOW TO QUIT YOUR JOB WITH PASSIVE INCOME"

FOR FREE!

Just to say thank you for buying this book, we'd like to give you the Cheat Sheet for "How to Quit Your Job with Passive Income"

100% FREE

DOWNLOAD FREE INSTANTLY HERE

http://www.masterpassiveincome.com/Passive-Income-Free-Offer

YOU CAN QUIT YOUR JOB WITH PASSIVE INCOME

Life was not meant to be lived in a cubicle!

In today's world, we all are expected to live our lives working for someone else. Working 40+ hours a week at a job you hate, for a horrible boss, and wasting your life away for a paycheck, is not how you should have to live your life. Fortunately, you found the book that will help you escape the rat race of life and ditch the cubical, assembly line, or dead end job.

How to Quit Your Job with Passive Income has been proven to help many people learn the secrets of passive income that only those who are already rich know. This book has been designed to help guide you through the process of being an employee earning a wage, to a business owner with multiple streams of passive income. This book is for people who suffer day-in and day-out in their J.O.B. or Just Over Broke.

As a lifetime student of business and passive income, and a master of the art of using passive income to quit my job, I've already quit my job and live solely off my passive income from my many businesses. Government employees, construction workers, financial analysts, self-employed business owners, and countless others who struggled with working a J.O.B. have already experienced great success with passive income by implementing the information found in this helpful how-to guide.

Sam, an ex-UPS employee says, "The best thing about the book is it can be read on Monday and are ready to jump into a business on Tuesday."

I promise that if you follow this how-to guide, you'll be able to start down the path of passive income and quit your job. AND I promise that if you implement the passive income strategies to your life, you'll make more money from your passive income than you ever could from a J.O.B. I will walk you step-by-step through the thought process and how you can change from having a poor employee mindset to a wealthy business owner mindset. You will learn that there is a difference between earned income and passive income as well as the proven ways you can change your life forever.

Don't be the person who misses out on opportunities in life because you are stuck in the same dead-end J.O.B. Be the kind of person other people marvel at saying: "I don't know how they do it but they are living the life of their dreams." The kind of person who sees opportunities in life and takes action immediately.

The passive income ideas in this book you are about to read have been proven to produce long-lasting results. I have already quit my job and you can too! All you have to do to make money with passive income is to keep reading. Each chapter will give new insight as you strive to build your passive income businesses.

Get ready for a lifetime of passive income where you have enough money to do the things you want to do without being dependent on anyone for a J.O.B. I encourage you to take the first step and start living the passive income life you were meant to live. Take control of your life right now, make the decision to quit wasting your life and start earning passive income today.

WHAT YOU WILL LEARN

How would you like to earn money while you are sleeping, on vacation, or playing with your kids? What if you could work one time and continually receive a paycheck every month?

This is exactly what passive income is all about. What you will learn in this book are the principles of passive income as well as the twelve proven types of passive income ideas you can use to quit your job. I have implemented the teaching in this book to quit my job. Once I found the power of passive income, I focused all my efforts learning as many passive income business models as possible.

There are many ways to earn passive income. One key to remember is that this book is NOT an end in itself. The main purpose of this book is to give you the tools and understanding to pursue passive income. The principles and ideas in this book will offer you a start down the road of passive income.

The chapter titled "12 Proven Ways to Earn Passive Income" and the subsequent chapters will provide you a general overview of each of the business models. Once you have decided on one or more of these to pursue, you need to devote yourself to becoming a master in it.

This book has different sections that build upon the one before it.

Section 1 "Foundation"

To understand how to make passive income we must first understand what it is and what it is not. This section is designed to help transform you from a regular employee into the world of passive income earners.

Section 2 "Breaking Out of a Broken System"

The system we have all grown to know about making money is broken. Anyone who has a job is at risk. This section will help you see how vital it is to have multiple streams of passive income.

Section 3 "Road Map"

You are your biggest obstacle to freedom without a job. Passive income requires a shift from a mindset of a poor person to the mindset of a rich person. This section will help you to change how you think about how you make, spend, and keep your money.

Section 4 "Investment Vehicle"

This is where the rubber meets the road, and you find out what are the proven ways to earn passive income. Even though there are many more ideas to earn passive income than described, these ways to earn passive income are proven to be successful.

Section 5 "Escape"

Once you have your path and vehicle picked out, it is time for you to start moving toward passive income and never look back. There are many things to consider when leaving your job and this is where you learn how to do it right.

Section 6 "Finish"

Now that you have gone through all the training, it is time for you to do it yourself. In this section, you will put together your plan to quit your job and live on your passive income.

SECTION 1
THE FOUNDATION

CHAPTER 1

YOU TOO CAN LIVE THE PASSIVE INCOME LIFE

"You measure the size of the accomplishment by the obstacles you had to overcome to reach your goals."

- Booker T. Washington

Life is better when you are not living in a cubicle, behind a counter taking orders, or even being a sole-proprietor grinding out each day to make a living. All of these have one thing in common. You work one hour, you get paid for one hour.

Wouldn't it be fantastic to work one hour and get paid hour after hour continuously? Wouldn't it also be fantastic to get paid while you are exercising, playing with your children, on vacation, or even sleeping? All these things are possible for you through passive income.

With a regular earned income job, your pay is specified by your employer. You agreed to work one hour for an hourly wage. The more hours you work, the more money you make. The problem is that you only have this one life and those hours you spend are precious. Is one hour of your life worth $15 an hour, $30 an hour, or even $100 an hour?

I guarantee you; the rich would gladly give all the money and possessions they had to live just a little bit longer. No one ever said on their death bed "I wish I worked more." Rather, they wish they had spent more time with their spouse, grandkids, or being with their loved ones. No matter how much money you make or what possession you acquire, you cannot take it with you when you die. In the end, your time is worth much more than any amount of hours you work.

Passive income is not just for the super-rich, for the incredibly smart, or even the hardest worker. It is for everyone who chooses to learn the process of passive income and have the fortitude to do everything they can to attain it. You can have the passive income life where you get paid even though you do not work another hour.

Think of passive income as the ability to earn money by doing something one time and continuously being paid over and over again. You work one hour and then continuously receive income for the work you did in that one hour. With passive income, the less you work, the more money you make. This is how the rich people of the world stay rich.

I can vouch for how amazing it is to live a passive income life. By working one time and being paid continuously after, I was able to quit my job. With passive income, I literally will never work another day for someone else again. Now, I do whatever I want, whenever I want and still earn enough money each month to live on.

Passive income can be a reality for you too. It will take hard work and determination to build up your passive income, but if you have the desire, you too can earn enough cash flow monthly from your passive income to quit your job.

WHAT PASSIVE INCOME IS

The term passive income has been thrown around a lot recently. People use it for things like multi-level marketing, starting a sole-proprietor business, and investing in the appreciation of stocks. The problem with these is that they are not passive. For something to be considered truly passive income, it has to fit the definition of both passive and income.

Passive: used to describe someone who allows things to happen or who accepts what other people do or decide without trying to change anything.

Income: money that is earned from work, investments, business, etc.

When you put these two together, you have someone who makes money without doing anything to earn it. The only work you do is when you start the passive income business. After that, the money comes in whether you work not.

If you want to quit your job, you need to replace your hourly/salary income with an income that comes in whether they do any work or not. Passive income allows you to get paid by the value you bring, not the hours you put in. If you have $3,500 in expenses per month and your passive income is $4,000 a month, you can quit your job and design your life the way you want to live it.

Since we all have monthly bills to pay, monthly cash flow from passive income is necessary to quit your job. Monthly cash flow from your passive income will allow you not to have to work while still paying your bills and covering your expenses.

The secret the rich know is how to spend their time and money acquiring assets. An asset is something that puts money in your pocket. Businesses, real estate, intellectual property, inventions, etc. are all assets that the rich acquire to earn themselves monthly cash flow. They don't work hourly jobs that earn them a wage. They own companies that employ people who make an hourly wage by working for them, making them even richer.

Passive income is a way for you not to have to work an hourly job again by bringing in monthly cash flow.

Cash Flow is King

Passive income is only income when it produces cash flow. The key to the term "passive income" is "income". Without income, all you have is the word passive, which will not pay your bills each month. The key principle to investing in passive income is that you receive income in the form of monthly cash flow.

Cash flow is the process of money coming into your pocket each month. Your paycheck can be considered cash flow since it is money that you receive every month. The problem with your paycheck is that you have to work to earn that cash flow. It is "income", but it is in no way "passive". The better way to cash flow is making money come in your pocket without you working at all.

With cash flow coming into your pocket each month, you can pay your bills, buy nice things, go on vacation, etc. Without it, you run the chance of going bankrupt and not losing everything.

Here are two examples of investing that show which one has cash flow or not.

1. Investing in real estate rental properties.

2. Buy cheap; sell high by investing in the stock market.

"Passive Income" with Cash Flow:

Only one of these will put money into your pocket each month that you can spend on whatever you want. The other is a way to hope that what you bought will go up in value so that you can sell it for a higher price to another person. It takes me about 3 hours to purchase a rental property, from beginning to end. After I have bought that property, I now have a cash flow producing asset that puts money into my pocket each month from the rents received.

If you are investing in something that does not bring in cash flow, it is not passive income. Buying stocks at a low price hoping that the value increases over time is not passive income. Without the regular distribution of cash into your pocket each month, this type of investment is speculating and does not bring income into your pocket.

One way to have a stock by passive income would be to purchase dividend paying stock that pays the shareholders from the company's proceeds and allows you to keep your ownership portion of the company. Then, you are paid out regularly with cash flow that you can spend as you desire.

Cash flow is best when you do not have to do anything to receive it.

WHAT PASSIVE INCOME IS NOT

Passive income is not trading hours for dollars.

When you have a job, you put in an hour of work and get an hour's worth of wages in return. Working a job is an example of trading hours for dollars. Being a sole proprietor of any business is also not passive income because you have to work every day to make money. If you don't service your customers, you don't get paid. You have substituted one boss for many different ones that can fire you whenever they want.

Earned income is simple: If you don't work, you don't get paid.

Passive income is not hoping something will appreciate in value. Putting your money in the stock market, mutual funds, treasuries, or bonds is not how to earn passive income. When you buy stock in a company, you are giving the company money in return for shares in the company. Those shares rise and fall on the earnings of the company, of which you have no control over. The officers and employees of the company have the control, leaving you hopeful that the earnings will go up over time and force the stock price to go up.

Stock investing for appreciation is not passive income. You only realize the money you gained or lost when you sell the stock. Likewise, with mutual funds; they are completely out of your control. There is a fund manager who pools investor's money together and purchased company stock in multiple different companies calling it a "diversified" portfolio.

On the other hand, a way to earn passive income from stocks is from those that pay a dividend each month. The profits from the company are paid to the owners of the stocks on a regular basis. This refers to passive income and cash flow.

Another example of passive income is writing a song that sells through iTunes. You write and record the song once, and then it is sold again and again easily and without any work on your end.

Passive income is only passive when it comes in without you doing any work to acquire it. Also, passive income is only income when it comes in regularly without you giving up your control of the asset.

PASSIVE INCOME IS NOT A GET RICH QUICK SCHEME

The very nature of passive income is that you get paid continuously for work you do only one time. If making passive income was quick and easy, everyone would be doing it. In reality, passive income involves hard work and a lot of patience.

It took me almost 10 years to earn enough passive income from my rental properties to replace the income from my J.O.B. (Just Over Broke).

To get a good idea of what passive income is, imagine you standing on the side of a large mountain. This mountain is totally covered in snow all the way down its 3000-foot face. Now, imagine yourself picking up a handful of snow with both your hands and packing it into a snowball.

Right now, this snowball is about the size of a baseball, and it is in your power to do with it what you want. You could set it back down and go on your way, or you can roll the ball down the side of the mountain. Passive income is just like that baseball size snowball. What you do with it will determine how big that snowball can grow. Since you are reading this book, you are the kind of person that wants to roll that snowball down the mountain to see how big it will get and how far it will go.

Now, imagine yourself rolling that snowball down the side of the mountain. At first, it moves slowly and grows little over time. After a little while, the ball doubles in size. The once baseball size snowball has become the size of a softball. Then, after even more time, that snowball becomes the size of a basketball.

As it keeps rolling down the mountain, it increases in both size and speed. After more time, the basketball-sized snowball becomes the size of a small car. Now the snowball is moving even faster and is gaining in size by the second. Because there is more surface area for the other snow to attach to, it gets bigger and bigger. Once the snowball is at this size, it is almost unstoppable.

Your passive income will be just like this snowball. At first, the progress will be slow, and the growth will be small. Over time, as you work hard to build up your passive income business, the speed and size will get larger and larger, just like the snowball.

Once you commit to a passive income life, you will be like that snowball. It will take time and hard work to get it to grow. But once you build it big enough, it will be almost unstoppable.

CHAPTER 2

HOW YOU WILL BENEFIT FROM PASSIVE INCOME

*"Opportunities don't happen,
you create them."*

- Chris Grosser

Practically, passive income is money you make while you are not working. Money coming in without working is a benefit of passive income that is easy to understand. But, what are other benefits of passive income? Think of all the things you could be doing if you were not spending your life working for someone else.

By working your way out of a job, you will now have the time to spend your life doing whatever you want. Along with doing whatever you want, there are many other huge benefits to passive income that may not be as easily understood until you experience it. These are just a few benefits of passive income when you quit your job.

YOU WILL NO LONGER WORK FOR MONEY TO PAY YOUR EXPENSES

For most people, the main reason to have a job is to make enough money to cover their expenses. If you had enough money coming in each month from your passive income to cover your expenses, what purpose would there be to have a job? It could be to make more money, but why keep working when you don't have to.

In my passive income business, I make more money per hour building my passive income business than I could ever earn from a job. Even though I have earned as much as $36 an hour, it still does not compare to the money I make when I buy one rental property (we will discuss this more later). With all my rental properties, I earn enough money from the rents to cover my expenses and have extra money left over.

Passive Income Builds On Itself

As you build your business, your hard work creating passive income will build on itself. The more money you make helps you to make more money. An example would be creating a business writing books. The more books you sell, the more it helps you sell additional books. The general idea is that a writer is a best seller because they sell a lot of books, and they sell a lot of books because they are best seller. The more books sold gets the book in front of more people which sells more books.

Another example of passive income building on itself is with real estate as rental properties. With one rental property you may earn $3,200 a year in rental income. If you don't spend that income, you now have another $3,200 the next year to buy another rental that will make you another $3,200 a year for a total of $6,400. Imagine if you have ten properties bringing in $32,000 each year. Your business becomes a snowball.

There is No Limit to How Much You Can Earn

Podcaster John Lee Dumas of Entrepreneur on Fire makes over $300,000 per year from his podcasting business. Author Steve Scott makes over $40,000 a month with his book writing business. Blogger Michelle Schroeder-Gardner made over $112,000 in one month from her blog business.

This is just the tip of the iceberg. There are so many other passive income business owners that make enough money to cover their expenses each month. With passive income, the sky is the limit. The longer you work on it, the more income you get from it. No boss is telling you they cannot give you a raise. You are now the boss.

You No Longer Have a Boss

Since you are working for yourself, you are now the boss. Ideally, your business is paying all of your expenses with some profit left over. With the extra profit, you can hire employees to do the things you do not want to do, or that do not make you enough money to spend your time on. Having your employees do all the work will allow you do the things that make you the most money that only you can do.

No longer having a boss is also freedom!

You no longer have to call in sick, ask for vacation time, or depend on him/her for a job. You are the master of your course now. No one is there telling you what to do. You are now in control of your life.

You Don't Have to Choose Just One Passive Income Business

A lot of the passive income business mesh well with the others. Say you are the creator of a blog, and you create great content for the world to consume. All of that content can be re-purposed into other businesses.

Take that great content you already have and turn it into a book you can sell on Amazon. Then, use the same content to create a podcast where you can earn money from sponsors and affiliate sales. What about YouTube? Create an awesome video that reaches a whole new audience with your content.

Real estate also has other forms of passive income connections. Create a blog teaching people how to make money in real estate. Borrow some of your money to other investors and earn interest just like a bank. Create a webinar that gives virtual walk-through of the business so you can teach more people.

The main takeaway is to put your eggs in multiple baskets. Focus your efforts on a few passive income businesses that complement each other and run with it.

You Stop Doing Things You Hate

Do you hate your job and would rather be working on your car? Are you stuck doing a job that you know your time would be much better spent doing other things? Would you rather be creating music that people could enjoy, than washing dishes?

When you have your own business with passive income, you don't have to be stuck doing the things you hate. If there is something you hate to do, just don't do it or hire someone else to do it. Life is too short to spend it doing things you hate.

You Do What You Love

They say if you do a job that you love, it no longer becomes work. If you are passionate about your job, it becomes a joy for you to do.

With passive income, you have the ability to choose what you want to do that fits your passions. Do you love to play the piano? Why not create a YouTube channel that teaches kids how to play the piano? Do you enjoy writing short stories? Why not put them together in a book and sell them on Amazon.

What about a passion for hiking up large mountains? Put together a blog that documents all your adventures and gives helpful hints and insights into your hiking.

The possibilities are endless. Here is a key: find what you are passionate about and match that up with one of the proven passive income ideas in this book.

You Set Your Hours and Work When You Want To

Being a business owner, the responsibility to work is solely on you. If you want to sleep in, do it. If you want to watch a movie at 2pm on a Tuesday, do it. Because you know what needs to be done in your business, you can work when you want to work.

If you are a night person and function better after 6pm than 6am, then start your work day at 6pm instead of 6am. If you have your passive income business built where it builds on itself, you don't even need to work.

In reality, you work when you want to and not work when you don't.

All of these reasons for passive income will hopefully fuel your desire to quit your job and invest your time in passive income businesses. Once you start, you will get the taste of the business and never want to stop.

You will be living the dream when you are living the passive income lifestyle.

CHAPTER 3

TIME TO LEARN SOMETHING NEW

"Getting rich begins with the right mindset, the right words, and the right plan."

- Robert Kiyosaki

TRADITIONAL EDUCATION TEACHES US TO BE EMPLOYEES

Since elementary school, we have all been taught one way to do things. We were given the knowledge (lecture and homework) to complete a task (test) and receive a reward (grade). This pattern is repeated all through our education in government schools. Teach, Study, Test and Reward. This model has shown each and every student essentially how to be an employee.

Every job is set up like this.

1. Orientation/Training

2. Test of Learned Skills

3. Complete tasks associated with the training

4. Earn money for tasks completed or total hours worked

The end goal of all education is to teach you how to be an employee. The government school system is structured in a way to give children the most knowledge so they can get the best job possible. This method is not necessarily a bad thing by any means. For most people, working a job their entire life is perfectly fine for them.

If you are reading this book, then you made the decision not to be one of those people who work for someone else making them rich. I took the decision back in 2006 to gain freedom from my job by earning passive income.

Passive income can be earned in different ways which we will take a look at in this book. I personally invest in real estate rental properties as my way to earn passive income. There are many other ways that you may find that are a better fit for you.

What passive income is can be summed up easily: Work once, get paid continuously.

Think about that.

You work one hour and you get paid again and again for what you did that one hour. When I purchase a rental property, I usually spend 2-3 hours in total acquiring the property. After I have already spent those hours, my rental property makes me money for the rest of the time that I own it.

Even when I am asleep, on vacation, playing with my kids, or watching TV, that one rental property is making me money from my 2-3 hours of work. Imagine if your boss kept paying you again and again for the 1 hour you work for him. This example is the beauty of passive income. You get paid continuously for the work you did one time.

I hate getting paid hourly.

I'd rather be paid for what I produce and create than the hour I work.

WHY THE RICH GET RICHER

Why do the rich get richer and the poor get poorer? It is not that the rich work harder than the poor. It is also not because the rich are smarter than the poor. You will find many smart, hard-working poor people who just do not know how to become and stay rich. The reason why the poor stay poor is because they have not learned how to become rich.

There are two things that you need in order to become rich:

1. Mindset to Being Rich and Staying Rich

2. The Path to Become Rich with Passive Income

Your mindset, and how you view yourself, is the first thing that must change to gain a passive income life. All of the conditioning you received since you were a child needs to be replaced with a mindset of being rich and staying rich. After you have the passive income life mindset, you need to find the right path to passive income that suits you.

There are many types of passive income out there to choose from. If you are not a songwriter or singer, don't worry. If you hate investing in the stock market, again, don't worry. There are numerous ways for you to earn passive income and you can choose how you want to spend your life.

Once you gain the mindset of being a passive income earner, you will never want to be an employee again. Once you have created your plan, you will become rich without ever working a job again.

In this book, we will go through a general overview of the different types of passive income streams that you can choose from. This will not be a full detailed "How To" for these topics. I have written other books that go much further into detail on the "How" in the passive income stream you choose.

After you start down the path of passive income, you will see how it is possible to quit your job because you have enough monthly cash flow coming to cover your expenses. Also, as you build your passive income business, it will build upon itself. Just like Steven King, who keeps writing more and more books, you will keep pursuing your passive income stream and build off the work you have already done.

CHAPTER 4

DISCOVER YOUR "WHY" TO HELP YOU QUIT YOUR JOB

"Sow a thought and you reap an action; sow an act and you reap a habit; sow a habit and you reap a character; sow a character and you reap a destiny".

– Ralph Waldo Emerson

The foundation of your passive income must start with the reason why you want to quit your job. By knowing your "why" you will have a reason to push through it when the road gets rough, and you begin to feel comfortable in the job you have.

Why do you want to quit your job?

Is it because you:

1. Don't want to have a boss
2. Hate your job
3. Desire to spend more time with your family
4. Believe that you are worth much more than your hourly wage

5. Want more money than you could ever make from a J.O.B.

6. You have a passion for something else that you want to devote your life to

No matter what your "why" is. It is up to you to find it and focus on it to change your future. When you sow the thought in your mind about your "why," you give yourself the ability to force yourself to change. This change in mindset is going to be the reason you need to help you stay on the path of passive income.

So, how do you discover your "why"?

Answer these five questions right now on a sheet of paper:

1. If you could snap your fingers and make your life perfect two years from now, what would it look like?

2. What do you do that makes you forget to eat because you are focused on finishing the task?

3. What are you doing right now that you never thought you would be doing when you were a child?

4. Bottom line, if you were to die 90 days from now, what would you be doing with your life?

5. How do you want to be remembered by your family, friends, and loved ones?

The way to understand your purpose in life and to discovering your "why" is to finding one, two, or three things in your life that get you out into the world and live. These are the reasons why you will move toward the life you always wanted to live.

Now that you have these written down, think of what your main purpose is.

Take time right now to figure out what your main purpose is and write it down with your answers to the questions above. Think of things bigger than yourself and how you can help more people. I cannot give you any examples of what your purpose could be because I am different than you. My purpose is most likely different than yours, and rightly so. We are all unique.

Even though we are all different, each and every one of us has a purpose. When we are fulfilling that purpose, we will be the most satisfied in our life.

Once you have these written down, put them in a place where you will be able to refer back to it in the future whenever you question the path of passive income. These questions will help you to stay focused on the end goal, not the hard work as you take the path least traveled.

YOU ONLY LIVE ONCE. BETTER MAKE IT COUNT FOR SOMETHING

This life is only lived once. Whether you live a good life or a bad one is really up to you. Your outlook and attitude towards this life will affect how you see the world and how the world sees you.

Your "why" must start with a change in you. This change must be to devote your life to something bigger than yourself. It must be something that changes you at the core so that the only thing you desire is your "why."

Something hit me a few years ago when my mother passed away from lung cancer. She was only 57 years old when she passed and had smoked for 15 years of her life. She quit 20 years before she died, but still got lung cancer.

My grandfather died of lung cancer when he was 58 years old. His brother too died of lung cancer when he was 56 years old.

When my mother died, I was 35 years old. I realized that I too, could die when I reach 57 years from lung cancer just like her. Then it hit me; I could only have 22 years left to live.

Death has a way to put things in perspective. The things that I thought were important weren't and the things I took for granted were the most important.

I say, "Praise the Lord" that I started building my passive income business when I was 26 years old because I knew there were greater things out there than working in a cubicle. Now that I have quit my job with passive income, I can now live life on my terms, not on someone who allows me to work for them.

If I only have 20 more years to live, why wouldn't I do everything in my power to quit my job and live the purpose God has given me while I am alive?

Quitting my job is the best decision I have ever made. Trust me; you will feel the same when you quit yours.

Remember, you only live once. Make this life count.

SECTION 2

BREAKING OUT OF A BROKEN SYSTEM

CHAPTER 5

FINANCIAL FREEDOM IS POSSI- BLE WITH PASSIVE INCOME

"If you always put limit on everything you do, physical or anything else. It will spread into your work and into your life. There are no limits. There are only plateaus, and you must not stay there, you must go beyond them."

- Bruce Lee

I have never liked working for anyone. Every job I had felt like a burden and one that I would easily give up if I had the chance. As I say that, I can see this statement can come across that I am someone who hates to work or even one who does not want to work. This statement is the furthest thing from the truth.

To me, work is fun. I enjoy "making" money, but I don't enjoy "earning" money. There is a difference.

Earning money is trading an hour of your life for money that comes from someone else. Making money is creating a means for you to make money out of nothing. You don't get paid for the hour you put in, but rather the value that you bring. This is essentially what passive income is.

Being an entrepreneur and a business owner, I am glad to give up my 40 hours a week job to work 80 hours a week for myself. This is because it is my business and I love what I do. If you love what you do, then it never feels like work.

Passive income is a shift from getting paid hourly, to getting paid continuously.

In 2004, I made the conscious choice to build my passive income business. I decided I was going to quit working for somebody else and live off passive income for the rest of my life. Honestly, it has not been easy. Actually, it is rather hard to build a passive income business that replaces your income. It takes time, dedication, and hard work.

The broken systems are:

1. Go to school and graduate

2. Go to college and graduate

3. Get a job at a big company

4. Work in the same job for 35 years

5. Retire at 65 with social security, pension, and your 401k

Back in the 1940's and 1950's, this was a good plan. Companies would hire and keep employees until they retired. The longer you worked for a company, the more money you made and the more retirement you made.

Companies were more loyal and they honored their long-lasting employees with very good benefits.

Since the year 2000 the culture of business has changed. Companies look more to the bottom line of their profit and loss statement and try to find ways to increase their profit. Sadly, the easiest way for them to do that is to cut their labor expense.

Employees are no longer viewed as a person but rather as a "tool". A "tool" that you can get rid of when it costs to much to maintain and does not produce what it had in the past. The company will try to find a new "tool" (employee) to replace the more expensive one.

Along with the problem of being discarded as a useless "tool", there is another glaring problem with this system. You only get paid once for the hour you work as an employee.

All of these statements are true if you are an employee:

1. If you do not work, you do not get paid

2. If your hours are cut, you work fewer hours and make less money

3. If you get fired from your job, you no longer have the means to earn money to pay your expenses

4. You are at the mercy of your boss who is in control over your time and life

5. If you leave your job, you cannot pay your bills

The passive income way of thinking is to own a business where you make money whether you work or not. You could be vacationing in Hawaii and still be getting paid without you doing a single thing. This idea is what got me thinking that passive income is the only true way to become wealthy and retire young.

CHAPTER 6

WHY YOU MUST PLAN YOUR ESCAPE: A REAL-LIFE EXPERIENCE

"Whenever you see a successful person you only see the public glories, never the private sacrifices to reach them."

- Vaibhav Shah

I received a phone call one day from my brother who worked for a fairly large corporation. He was the corporate office manager for a company that owned restaurants. He worked his way up from a server in the restaurant to the assistant manager, and then became the general manager.

After working as a general manager for four years, he moved into the position of office manager. He really enjoyed the change because being a general manager of a restaurant you work long hours, nights, weekends, and even holidays. Since moving to the corporate office, he was now able to work "regular" hours of 8 AM to 5 PM with holiday vacations and nights off. He enjoyed his job and did very well at it.

After a few years working in the corporate office, the corporation decided it was time to sell the entire business and was listed for sale. Selling a big company that owns multiple restaurants does take some time for the sale to finalize. The employees of the company my brother worked for didn't know when the sale was supposed to go through or even if it would go through. On August 20th, 2015 the sale finalized and a new, larger corporation owned the company that my brother worked for.

I received a call from my brother at 10 AM the morning of the sale. He called to let me know that he had just been fired from his job and the new corporation was "cleaning the house" by firing all the corporate employees. He shared the little detail he knew about the employees being fired and we speculated the reason why they were all fired. After the shock of being fired from his job, we both talked about plans to create passive income from businesses to help him not to have to work again.

The main point of all this is that if you work for someone else, you are dependent on them providing you with a job. That job allows you to provide for you and your family. At any given moment, your employer can decide to fire you for whatever reason. If you are at the whim of an employer, you are standing on a ticking time bomb, ready to blow. I have personally worked hard for the past nine years to get myself away from being dependent on anyone.

A RUDE AWAKENING THAT OPENED MY EYES

Most people are not prepared when the time comes that they may be fired or be let go from their job. In today's world, it is not "if" you get fired or laid off, but "when". For eight years, I believed I would never be laid off. I was a hard worker, had good seniority, worked for a local government agency, and the economy had begun to grow again.

In 2012, after working for the same government organization for eight years, I received a two-week layoff notice. I was laid off because the department I was working for was subjected to a statewide lawsuit that cut $1 million a year into their budget from loss of revenue. The department needed to cut back on expenses, and the "elected" official decided to lay off everyone who stood their ground against the wrong things he was doing.

Even though I had been working hard for the previous eight years building up my passive income to quit my job, I did not feel like I was ready to stop working. It seemed like it was mostly because I had not planned my escape yet because I figured I could work for a few more years. That, coupled with the fact that my rental properties were not as consistent in bringing in enough monthly cash flow for our family to live on.

When I got the layoff notice, I just had my fourth child who was barely two months old. My first week back from paternity leave, the "elected" official gave me a two week layoff notice. Because I didn't feel I was ready to stop working, I went out and beat the pavement to find another job. Praise the Lord; I found another job in the County government within one week of receiving a layoff notice. This was because I had an excellent reputation in the entire county government as being smart, a hard worker, and a strong leader. The great thing was that I was able to find a fantastic job with the same pay, seniority, benefits, etc. So, I was never technically laid off because I transferred to my new job before the layoff date arrived.

Going through the experience of being laid off and not feeling like I was prepared was an eye-opener. It solidified in my mind that I need to plan my escape from working as quickly as possible. As long as I was working for someone else, they would have power over me because they could take my job away from me whenever they want.

CHAPTER 7

MY PATH TO GAIN FINANCIAL FREEDOM WITH PASSIVE INCOME

"Success is walking from failure to failure with no loss of enthusiasm."

- Winston Churchill

My brother and I started a retail establishment in 2006 called Downtown Express in Downtown Fresno CA. Downtown Express was a convenience store and pizzeria combination that catered to the employees that worked in the downtown area. Our goal was to create a business that employed people to work for us while we collected the profit.

For a few years, the business was doing very well. We were making money and the economy was strong. Then, in 2009, the economy crashed, and our business began a steady decline in sales and profits. The main problem was that employees were losing their jobs all around us because the economy was failing. Employees were laid off, some had their hours reduced, and even some had their salaries reduced.

This situation left fewer and fewer employees as customers for our business. Without customers, the business was no longer generating money. Instead, we were putting our money into the company. For a business like this to be a passive income business, you need to have employees run it while you pay them for the hour they worked. They were the ones being paid by the hour, and I was making money from their work.

There are two ways you can run a business. The first is to be a sole proprietor and work in the business every day. A sole proprietor is a person who would work in the business on a day to day basis and does not hire employees. With this business model, you now "own" a job. If you do not work, then you do not make money. You have basically traded one boss for many. Each customer is now your boss.

The second is to be a business owner and employ others to run your business. The beautiful thing about this is if you aren't working, your employees are. They are making you money because they are working, while you are not. For Downtown Express, I ran this business as a business owner, not a sole proprietor. I oversaw the business and had my employees run it.

My goal was to make Downtown Express a successful business that I would be able to grow into a profitable company. I wanted to build a company that would employ people to work "in" the business while I worked "on" the business. Essentially, I had the desire to control the business and allow others to make money for me.

As the economy got worse in 2009, so did the sales from the business. As we made less money, it became more difficult to pay our payroll, let alone earn any money. Being that the business was in downtown Fresno, the store hours were from 7 am to 5 pm, Monday through Friday because that was when the employees worked. If there were no employees working downtown, there would be no sales and we would not make any money; so we closed on the weekends and at nights. It later hit me that I was paying 24 hours of rent to my landlord for the lease but only making money in only a few of those hours.

After owning the business for four years, I decided to sell it. The economy was in recession, and it did not seem like we were going to make a profit through the route we were going. It seemed as though the wisest decision would be to sell and get out of the retail business. I did not want to own a job by being a sole proprietor working in the business; so I sold everything. My financial freedom would have to wait.

What I could have done was quit my job, work on my business for 50 to 60 hours a week and fire all my employees but then I would be trading one job for another. My goal was to have passive income, not earned income.

The process of owning a failing business and then selling it was truly a rough experience, but one that I would not give up. The entire process of starting a business to selling it was a way for me to learn and earn practical experience that I would probably never get from a university having a Master's degree in Business.

I did also learn that I do not ever want to own a retail business again. Some people are great at retail businesses. I just know that I am not one of those people.

CHAPTER 8

THE PASSIVE INCOME BUSINESS I USE TO GAIN FINANCIAL FREEDOM

"The starting point of all achievement is desire."

- Napoleon Hill

While I was building and running Downtown Express, I began to invest in real estate buying them as rental properties. This was a new type of business I had never had any experience with. When I started it, it seemed easy enough. Buy a property, fix it up, find a tenant to pay you monthly rent, and then let the property do all the work.

Theoretically, this is the entire business model summed up in one sentence. Practically, there is much more that goes into building a passive income business in real estate. As I began to build this new business, I realized that this is the most passive way I could find to make money and earn a substantial monthly cash flow to quit my job.

Each property I purchased made me money even though I did not work a single hour on them. Once the property was purchased, I had my property manager do all the work, and I just collected the rent checks each month.

As I saw the returns from the rental properties increase and multiply with each new property, it became even more solidified in my mind that rentals were the best way to earn passive income and invest my money.

> **The best thing about rental properties is that they work for me 24 hours a day 365 days a year making me money.**

That is financial freedom.

In my real estate business, I do not work on the properties or even manage them. All of the properties that I own have a Property Manager (PM) who manages them. Even if the properties are in the same city that I live in, I still hire a PM. This is because I don't want to deal with managing properties; I just want to be an investor who makes money from the properties.

For the ultimate passive income, I have Property Managers (PM) do all the work for me. The PM handles the cleanup, renting, collecting rents, evictions, and everything in between for each of the properties. They are my employees, and I pay them well for doing it.

In 2007, I bought my first rental property in Ohio. Even though I live in Fresno California, I wanted to find the highest return for my money each month. My goal was to replace my earned income with passive income, so I found an area of the country that had the lowest priced house I could find with the highest rent amount each month.

I decided to invest in Ohio because of the great rate of return on the properties compared to California where I live. I would have a cash flow of $450 each month from only $15,000 invested into the property, and I owned them without a mortgage.

In CA, I could buy a $250,000 home, earn $100 a month, and have a monthly mortgage payment of $1,500. If I have one eviction, I would be without a renter for two months or more. The carrying costs could be $3,000 as well as cleaning and renting the property. I could have $3,500+ out of my pocket for that one eviction. In one year, I would only earn $1,200 cash from the rents which would be wiped out with one eviction.

With the properties in Ohio, I pay an average of $12,000 per home and have it rented for $550 per month with little to no mortgage payment. Since this business was so lucrative, I reinvested all the income I made from the business back into it to buy more properties.

HOW I GOT STARTED WITH RENTAL PROPERTIES

After my first property was rented and producing a good monthly cash flow, I decided to refinance it and pulled out money to buy my second property. The mortgage payment is only $150 per month, and I was able to buy a second property that earned $550 each month in rent. Both of these rentals were single family homes that produce $550 in rent every month.

I paid $17,000 cash for the first and $15,000 cash for the second for a total of $32,000 and earned $1,100 in rent each month. I was able to pocket about $850 each month after expenses and the payment of the note on the first property.

Once the second property was rented and producing cash, I refinanced it to pull out money to invest in more rentals. From refinancing the second property, I was able to buy two properties and had a total of four rental properties that produced $2,100 per month in rent. The cash flow on those four properties is $1,800 a month which is the passive income that I earn by not doing a thing.

Since I was pulling in $1,800 a month in passive income from such little work, I decided that was the investment idea I would stick with. I saved all the money I earned from the rents and used it to buy more properties. Each year after that, I purchased three and sometimes even four properties in one year.

After nine years of investing in rental properties, I had 24 rental properties and enough passive income from these properties that I could quit my job. These rental properties bring cash flow every month as a means of income that I can replace the earned income from my job.

THE ROAD MAP TO PASSIVE INCOME

CHAPTER 9

DEVELOP AND MASTER A PASSIVE INCOME MINDSET

"You must expect great things of yourself before you can do them."

- Michael Jordan

There are many people in the world today that are just fine with being an employee. Most likely you are not one of them.

If you are reading this right now, then you are one of the few people that dare to go against the conventional wisdom that you must have a J.O.B. With the J.O.B., you are taught that your employer, 401k, or the government will take care of you in your retirement.

The first step down the path to financial freedom and quitting your J.O.B. is to understand how your mindset will determine how you act. If you believe that you are an investor, then your entire outlook on life will change to that of an investor. If you feel you are only good enough to be an employee at Burger King, then that is all you will ever be.

A strong master passive income mindset is what you need to quit your J.O.B. with passive income. Being able to tell yourself that you are not an employee but a business owner and investor will allow you to see a new possible future for yourself. It sounds somewhat cliché', but you can do anything you put your mind to.

With a master passive income mindset, the sky is the limit for the amount of money you can make AND how you can make that money. Once you get the taste of passive income, you will want as much of it as you can get. With a poor person's mindset, you will believe that you were always meant to be poor and always will be.

From this point forward, imagine yourself already as a millionaire. As a millionaire, you would have a drastically different way you see the world. You would see how everywhere you look there is an opportunity to earn money through passive income. You would have millionaire friends, millionaire ideas, millionaire contacts and business partners, and even millionaire possessions.

Do you think Donald Trump, Bill Gates, Warren Buffet, or Mark Cuban hang out with people who make minimum wage? Do they think about how they can get a raise in their job so they can buy a better car? Do they worry about their retirement and if they will have enough money when they are old? The answer is 'no' to all of these questions.

The only thing you can change about yourself right now is to have a master passive income mindset. Passive income opportunities are everywhere, and are waiting for you. Everywhere and everyone is a potential means to an idea that will bring you freedom from your job.

Once you start thinking how to get out of the rat race of life, you will eventually find a way.

They say that necessity is the mother of invention. Well, if you were fired from your job now, and you knew you needed to make money to pay your bills, you would use your mind to figure out a way to earn or make money in order to pay your bills.

Picture yourself right now without a J.O.B. and still had your same bills and obligations. You would get creative and find ways to make money. It could be through getting a new job, to starting a small business that brings in income on the side. Either way, when you are forced to think your way out of a problem, usually you find the solution.

There are four principles of a passive income mindset that you need if you want to ever quit your job.

1. Pay Yourself First

2. Control Your Expenses

3. Make Your Money Work For You

4. Work One Time and Get Paid Continuously

PAY YOURSELF FIRST

The first mindset change you need is to "Pay Yourself First". What this means is for you to make sure you keep 10% of what you earn from your job for yourself. For every $100 that you take home, you keep in for yourself $10. This money is to be saved and not spent on anything that does not make you money. By paying yourself first 10% of your income, after time, your bank account balance will grow larger and larger.

What you must remember is not to buy anything with this money because that does not make you money. New cars, big TV's, vacations, etc. are all types of items that take money out of your account, but do not put any back. If you spend this saved money on things that do not make you money, you are thinking like a poor person. A rich person looks to purchase assets that put money in their pocket each month, not take it out.

To start the process of paying yourself first, you may need to start small and work your way up to 10%. If you are not in the habit of saving money now, start with taking out 1% of your gross pay and saving it in a bank account for future use. This would equate to $20 a month if you currently earn $2000 a month. Month after month, increase the % by 1% until you reach 10%. After ten months, you will be saving $200 a month in your bank account to be put to use investing in anything that makes money for you.

Income: $2000 a month

Month 1: $20	Total Saved: $20
Month 2: $40	Total Saved: $60
Month 3: $60	Total Saved: $120
Month 4: $80	Total Saved: $200
Month 5: $100	Total Saved: $300
Month 6: $120	Total Saved: $420
Month 6: $140	Total Saved: $560
Month 7: $160	Total Saved: $720
Month 8: $180	Total Saved: $900
Month 10: $200	Total Saved: $1,100
Month 11: $200	Total Saved: $1,300
Month 12: $200	Total Saved: $1,500

After one year of paying yourself first, you would have $1,500 saved for you to invest in an income producing asset. This asset will pay you a monthly cash flow that you will use to replace your income. What would happen if you kept paying yourself first for the next year?

Month 1: $200	Total Saved: $1,700
Month 2: $200	Total Saved: $1,900
Month 3: $200	Total Saved: $2,100
Month 4: $200	Total Saved: $2,300
Month 5: $200	Total Saved: $2,500
Month 6: $200	Total Saved: $2,700

Month 6: $200	Total Saved: $2,900
Month 7: $200	Total Saved: $3,100
Month 8: $200	Total Saved: $3,300
Month 10: $200	Total Saved: $3,500
Month 11: $200	Total Saved: $3,700
Month 12: $200	Total Saved: $3,900

After two years of paying yourself first, you would have $3,900! If you continued paying yourself first for another year, you would have enough money for a down payment on a house!

Do you see the power of paying yourself first?

It is the power to have enough cash to take advantage of opportunities that you would not normally have had the cash to move on. If you are currently living in an apartment, why not buy a house for yourself to live in, so you are not throwing away money each month on rent? When you own a house and have a mortgage, you are paying off the purchase price of the property and putting your old rent money into your house.

Your home is now a means for you to keep your money rather than give to a landlord.

With the discipline of paying yourself first, the money that you gain over time will be a way for you to buy real assets that pay you money on a monthly basis. As you start to pay yourself first, over time, you will be amazed at how much money you will have and be at your fingertips. No more living paycheck to paycheck.

Remember, do not spend this money on anything that does not make you money each month in passive income. If you purchase an asset with this money, you are thinking like a rich person and earning cash flow each month.

CONTROL YOUR EXPENSES

The second principle is to "control your expenses". This is living below your means and not spending more than 90% of your earnings. The only real way to do this is to list out exactly what your expenses are each month, and then cut out costs to get you below 90% of your income.

Notice what this principle is not. It is not that you should "cut" your expenses. It does say to "control your expenses". Everyone will have expenses in their life. Some people may even have higher expenses than others. The total dollar amount of your expenses is not the concern. The concern is how it compares to how much money you bring in.

Your expenses should not exceed 90% of your income for two reasons. Firstly, you will not be paying yourself first and secondly, you may even be going into debt buying things that do not bring you income in the form of monthly cash flow.

To have more money in your pocket that you can save for investing, you need to either increase income or decrease expenses. Cutting expenses is hard to do but must be done for you to be rich. We will talk about how to increase your income in a later chapter. Right now, we need to understand how to control spending. More specifically, try not to spend more money than 90% of your income.

If you are currently living paycheck to paycheck or on credit cards, this step is crucial for you to gain a passive income mindset. Wealthy people do not live off credit cards. They do not live paycheck to paycheck. They live below their means and do not overspend on anything. You would be surprised how frugal most wealthy people are.

In today's media, we see the ridiculously rich of the world live lavish lives and spend ridiculous amounts of money. Well, most wealthy people are not like that. They are wealthy because they do not overspend and they save their money. Many wealthy people drive older vehicles, live in normal houses, and even pick up change they see on the street.

Tim Farris, in his book "Four Hour Work Week" talks about the "New Rich" of the world. These are people who have learned how to live a life free from a J.O.B. and can enjoy life as they decide it should be. The new type of rich people are those who do not have to work for a living, spend time with their family, enjoy their spouse, and live a normal life free of the cares of a job.

If you control your expenses to be 90% of your income, you are well ahead of most population. By only spending 90% of your income and saving the other 10% for the purchase of income producing assets, you will be one of the "New Rich."

CHAPTER 10

HOW TO IMPLEMENT THESE FIRST TWO PRINCIPLES TO QUIT YOUR JOB

"Success is the sum of small efforts,
repeated day-in and day-out."

- Robert Collier

To understand how you can quit your job in ten years, you need to look at your income and expenses and plan accordingly. If your income is high and your expenses are also high, it will be hard to save money and invest it. If you are going into debt every year, then you will never escape your job because you are tied down to it. Many have high paying J.O.B.s (Just Over Broke), possibly making $100,000 a year in wages, but they have expenses that are just as high as their income.

Their standard of living matches their income so they will always have to work the same J.O.B. year after year just to make ends meet. Likewise, if you have a lower paying J.O.B. making $40,000 a year in wages and have expenses of $40,000 or more every year, you are just treading water, not getting anywhere. You must work year after year, just like the person earning $100,000 a year.

Think of this scenario and ask yourself who is richer between John and Katie:

John	Katie
Yearly Salary: $100,000	Yearly Salary: $40,000
Yearly Expenses: $120,000	Yearly Expenses: $35,000
Annual Savings: -$ 20,000	Annual Savings: $5000
Starting Savings: $ 5,000	Starting Savings: $0
Starting Debt: $0	Starting Debt: $0

John, who is following the way most poor people go, has a yearly salary of $100,000 and has $120,000 per year in expenses. His focus is on "living in the now" by living paycheck to paycheck. All his money plus what he borrows on his credit cards goes to lavish vacations, expensive cars, mortgages, etc.

After five years, John still has his $100,000 yearly salary and kept the same expenses and added annual debt of $20,000 for a total debt of $100,000 after the five years.

Katie, who wants to start investing in real estate, has a yearly salary of $40,000 and has $35,000 per year in expenses. Her focus is living for the future and saving her money for passive income. All her money goes to the payment of her few bills while she's wise with her money, by living in a home she can afford, going camping for vacations, driving a 15-year-old car she bought for $3,000 cash 5 years ago. She works hard to control her expenses and keep them below the income she makes from her J.O.B. She also knows she needs to pay herself first and saves $5,000 a year to be invested in passive income ideas.

Katie is able to save $5,000 a year to invest in passive income, which brings her cash flow each month through real estate. She can save for one year, buy a home with an FHA mortgage with only 3.5% down and rent it out with positive cash flow of $300 per month. Each year, she does it over and over again, keeping her same expenses, but increasing her passive income and monthly cash flow.

In my opinion, even though John makes more money from his earned income, his expenses are so high that he is really poor. He will be forced to work his job every day for the rest of his life to live and pay off the debt that he's incurred. Katie, on the other hand can save money and escape from her job by investing in rental properties to replace her earned income with passive income.

LET'S LOOK AT KATIE'S NUMBERS

Let's look at Katie numbers:

Income: $50,000

Expenses: $45,000

Savings: $5,000

Katie is able to save $5000 a year because she spends less than she earns. With that money, she will be able to invest in items that bring her monthly passive income. If she is wise, she will keep her expenses low, and she will continue to save the $5000 a year. This savings plus any money she earns from her investments will allow her to continue to purchase more and more investments.

Here is an example of how she will be able to increase her income in five years by $18,000 with rental properties.

After purchasing one rental property that earns her $300 a month which is $3,600 a year, she now has an annual income of $53,600 a month. ($50,000 + $3,600 = $53,600) If she then saves that extra $300 a month, instead of spending it, she will now have $8500 from one year of saving to put towards another rental property that will make her even more money. (Remember, she is already saving $5,000 a year from her job)

Now, in her third year of investing, she purchases another rental property that brings in $300 a month. She now has two properties that pay her an extra $600 a month which is $7,200 per year increase to her total income.

If Katie continues to purchase one property each year after that, she will have enough passive income in five years to earn $14,400 per year on top of her regular income. By investing in rental properties, this scenario is entirely possible.

Here is the breakdown:

Year 1: One rental property at $300 a month = $3,600 yearly income

Year 2: Saving only. No properties purchased

Year 3: Two rental properties at $300 a month = $7,200 yearly income

Year 4: Three rental properties at $300 a month = $10,800 yearly income

Year 5: Four rental properties at $300 a month = $14,400 yearly income

After five years investing in rental properties, Katie now earns an extra $14,400 a year in PASSIVE INCOME!

It is not easy and does take hard work and patience. But if you are determined, you can be just like Katie and purchase one home per year with your savings.

For Katie, if she continues her current path of acquiring one property per year for the next seven years, at year 15, she would have 14 properties and earn $50,400 each year in passive income. Her passive income now surpasses her monthly salary from her J.O.B. If she wanted to, she could then retire and live off her income for the rest of her life.

This case is just one scenario, and rental properties are just one way to earn passive income. There are many other ways out there that you can earn true passive income. We will get to all these in a bit.

CHAPTER 11

MAKE YOUR MONEY WORK FOR YOU

*"Only put off until tomorrow
what you are willing to die
having left undone."*

- Pablo Picasso

For most people in the world, they are the employee. They are hired by someone else to make money for them. This one employee agrees to be paid a wage in return for an hour of their life. If you own a business that had employees, you will make money from your employees. The small downside is that you have to pay your employees for the work they performed.

Imagine if you have a business where you had employees, but you didn't have to pay them to work for you. A business where your employees make you money while you sleep, on vacation, play with your kids, etc. would be a good business to own!

This is the principle of making your money work for you. Think of each of your dollars as a little employee that works day and night for you. The more of these little employees you have, the more work they can do for you and the more money you will make.

An easy example would be a savings account at a bank. If you were to put in $1000 into a savings account at a bank, the bank would give you interest for using your money. As the bank lends out your money to other people at a higher interest rate, it pays you an interest rate (much lower than it receives when it lends it out to other people).

While your money is in the savings account, it accrues interest from the bank, and the bank pays you an interest payment on a regular basis for the money borrowed and lent to others. This example is a type of passive income that makes your money work for you.

On a much larger scale, an example of having your money work for you is the example of Katie who saved her money to purchase rental properties. Every penny she puts into her rental property business is another employee that will work hard for her day and night.

There are many other ways to have your money work for you. By investing in a company stock that pays a regular dividend to its shareholders, your money invested in that stock is hard at work for you. Or, by lending your money to someone else that will pay you interest on that money, your money will be working for you day and night earning you interest.

From this point forward, think of your money as an employee that you can put to work. If you spend your money on items that do not bring you money, then you are giving away your employees for nothing. Let's say you purchase a new LED TV. It is one of the biggest in the store and costs $2500. This TV will not make you any money. Also, once you spend that money, you no longer own it. While this purchase may be worth-while, it is not making you any money but only costing you money.

By making your money work for you, you are putting them to work. You still own the money, and it may just be in the form of a house you purchased and are renting out to earn a monthly cash flow of passive income.

CHAPTER 12

WORK ONCE AND GET PAID CONTINUOUSLY

*"Too many of us are not living
our dreams because we
are living our fears"*

- Les Brown

What do you think would happen if you asked your boss if he would continually pay you every month for your one hour of work? He would laugh you out of his office, right? I sure would laugh at one of my employees if they asked that question.

Passive income is not a boss. You are the boss with passive income. You get paid based on the amount of effort you put into your passive income business. As you devote your time to building streams of passive income, you can determine what is worth your time or not. Say you had a choice to spend one hour of your life in two different ways:

1. Making an item that you can earn a one-time profit of $100

2. Writing a song that will be sold for $.99 continuously every day for the next ten years

While both of these have a good outcome of income, the second way will bring you money continuously for the next ten years. After 101 days, you have already surpassed the $100 item and will continuously bring you money well beyond that.

Book Writing

The famous author Steven King utilizes the principle of working one time and getting paid continuously. Every day, he forces himself to write 2000 words for his next book. If it takes him 3 hours to write 2000 words, and a normal King book is about 300,000 words, he will write a new book in a total of around 450 hours. From those 450 hours, he will make at minimum $1,000,000 on his new book from the sales.

$1,000,000 for 450 hours of work is $2,222 per hour! Now that is just the start of it all. His books will be for sale for as long as anyone buys books so he will continually be earning passive income from the 450 hours of work until he dies. On top of that, each new book he writes earns him another $1,000,000and helps his other books to sell more too!

Patent and Licensing

Another idea is for you to create a product that can be patented and leased to another company. Imagine if you were the person who came up with the idea of the post-it note. Those are the little yellow sticky pieces of paper that all offices in the world use.

Create the product one time, patent it and then license it to another company to manufacture, distribute, and sell the product. You already did the work and now your product is working all on its own for you. No more work is required on your part since your work was done creating the product and you now own the patent.

Rental Properties

How do you think most millionaires made their wealth? Andrew Carnegie said "90% of all millionaires became so through owning real estate".

From my own personal experience with real estate, I can absolutely agree with this quote. All of my rental properties make me money month after month. In fact, there are _5 ways rental properties make me money_.

1. Net Profit Valuation in Cash Flow
2. Equity Capture
3. Appretiation
4. Equity Buildup
5. Tax Advantages

You are probably now realizing the power of working once and getting paid continuously. This principle is crucial to passive income. There is work on the front end while you build your passive income business, but eventually it will run itself if you build it right.

These are just a few examples of how to use passive income to quit your job. As you keep reading, you will learn many more ways to earn passive income to quit your job.

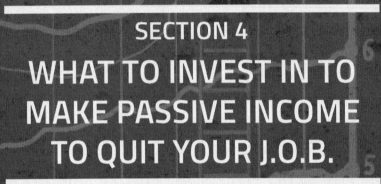

SECTION 4

WHAT TO INVEST IN TO MAKE PASSIVE INCOME TO QUIT YOUR J.O.B.

CHAPTER 13

FIND YOUR INVESTMENT VEHICLE

*"A real entrepreneur is somebody
who has no safety net
underneath them."*

- Henry Kravis

So, how do you pick the passive income ideas that will allow you to be financially free?

Getting started is taking one step in the direction you want to go and making small course corrections as you are going along the path. I have made many small course corrections in my life as I have worked towards building my passive income to quit my job.

What about you? If you want to be financially free, where do you begin? What investment vehicle are you going to take to retire? Are you going to invest in stocks, mutual funds, real estate, businesses, or online businesses, writing books, etc.?

I believe the entire goal of quitting your job is to have the time to do what you want, and not what someone else tells you to do.

To get started finding the right investment vehicle for you, begin to think about what you love to do. Do you love helping other people learn something new? Do you love to work with your hands around your house? Do you enjoy coming up with and writing short stories? Are you a master at fishing?

Think about what you love to do and then try to figure out how you can make passive income from it. I love to help people learn new things that will help them grow. I am also very passion about real estate and everything about it. So, rental properties and book writing are two things that I enjoy doing, so it doesn't feel like work.

Only you know what you are passionate about and what you love to do. The trick is to make money from that passion in the form of passive income.

One example would be a man who loves to fish. He knows everything about types of fish, what bait to use, where to fish, how to learn new locations, etc. He is not an expert but has a passion for it. A perfect fit for passive income would be to teach others everything he knows through blogs, podcasts, book writing, etc.

The key is to take all that passion and focus it on helping reach as many people as possible. The goal would be to help as many people as possible learn how to be a successful fisherman.

Let's now look at twelve proven passive income generating businesses you can focus your passions on.

CHAPTER 14

12 PROVEN WAYS TO EARN PASSIVE INCOME

I f you do a search through any search engine, you will find many sites giving you a list of passive income ideas that you can use. The problem is that most of these "ideas" are not passive income. The majority of them require you to continually do work in order to make money. Here are some examples these sites will use:

1. Use cash back rewards on credit cards

2. Earn money when you search online

3. Freelance your skills

4. Sell handmade products on Etsy

5. Enter contests and giveaways

6. Search for freebies online

7. Sell your collectibles

8. Get cash back when buying online

Do you see why these are not passive income? You actually have to do something to have the benefit come back to you. If you become a freelance writer, you get paid for what you write one time, just like a job.

These are not passive income.

As we have seen before, passive income is true when it is BOTH passive with little or no work by you and has income in the form of cash flow.

There are twelve proven ways for you to make passive income to quit your job. The beautiful thing about each of these is that you can do the majority of them at the same time! You don't have to be a "One Trick Pony" where all you have is one business that produces passive income. With these twelve proven passive income ideas, you will be able to quit your job quicker than you ever thought possible.

Now I must say that for each of these twelve proven passive income ideas, going into detail on how to effectively run these businesses are way out of the scope of this book. If you want more detail on these, I have much more information for you on how to do this on my blog _www.masterpassiveincome.com._ There, you will find blog posts, online courses, books, and other resources on how you can quit your job with these passive income ideas.

Let's jump into the top twelve proven passive income strategies you can do to quit your job. Remember, you can do more than one of these at a time. In fact, I encourage you to do at least three or more!

CHAPTER 15

BUSINESS MODEL OF INVES-
TING MONEY INTO A BUSINESS

"Try not to become a person of success, but rather try to become a person of value."

-Albert Einstein

1. Investing in Real Estate

- **Financial Risk: Moderate –** Can be lessened to "Low" with education
- **Financial Reward: Moderate –** Can be increased to "High" with education
- **Financial Liquidity: Very Low**
- **$ Requirement: Low to Very High**
- **Time Commitment: Very Low -** If you use a property manager

This method of investing in real estate is to buy a property and rent it to a tenant who pays you a monthly rent. In my opinion, this type of passive income is one of the best ways to earn passive income. It is the way I earn enough money to have already quit my job. With rental properties, your property does all the work and you reap the benefits. Once you own the property, it will keep working for you while you collect the rent checks.

The rent you charge should cover all of your expenses and mortgage payment and leave you cash flow after all the expenses are paid. Once you buy the house, fix it up to be rent-ready, employ a property manager who will rent out the property and maintain it, and you're done. Now all you need to do is collect your rent check from the property manager each month. Your money is working for you in your property in five different ways.

Now, creating a rental business sound is simple, but it does take a good amount of knowledge to make money in this business. It is very easy to lose money if you do not know what you are doing. I have documented all this for you on my blog www.masterpassiveincome.com. You can read all my posts on it for free.

Extra Resources: If you want to learn more in depth on how to quit your job with rental properties, I encourage you to check out my book **"How to Quit Your Job with Rental Properties: A Step-by-Step Guide to Unlocking Passive Income Investing In Real Estate"** It will give you my blueprint on how I quit my job with rentals. You can find it through my website at www.masterpassiveincome.com/thebook/

2. Lending Money to Earn Interest

■ **Financial Risk: Moderate to High**

■ **Financial Reward: Low**

■ **Financial Liquidity: Very Low**

■ $ Requirement: High

■ Time Commitment: Low

Lending money to others is basically like being a bank. You are making loans to others who guarantee the repayment of the principle, plus the agreed upon interest.

If you desire to earn passive income from the money you already have, this may be an option for you. Usually, the returns are anywhere from 7% to 15% depending on how you lend your money. Since you are the lender, it is up to you to come up with the interest rate you are willing to lend your money for.

Just like a bank who makes up the rate they are willing to lend, you have the option to lend your money or not and for a specified amount. Also, you need to find someone who is willing to borrow your money at your specified interest rate.

The new trend in lending is social lending. This is a platform where websites pair up individuals who would like to lend their money for a return to borrowers who are willing to pay interest to borrow their money. The website earns money from the transactions they set up between the borrowers and buyers.

Since I have never used any of these sites, I cannot recommend any of them. When I have any extra money, I put it into real estate rental properties.

To find social lending sites, just do a quick search for them and take your pick.

3. Investing to Gain Interest

a. Bank Savings Account

- **Financial Risk: Extremely Low** – Extremely unlikely you will lose your money

- **Financial Reward: Extremely Low** – Currently earn .010% monthly on average

- **Financial Liquidity: Extremely High** – You can take your money out very easily

The definition of interest is: money paid regularly, at a particular rate for the use of money lent, or for delaying the repayment of debt. By that definition, there are many possible ways to get paid regularly with your money.

The simplest form of interest would be to put your money in a bank savings account. Usually, this is the lowest amount of interest you can earn from your hard earned money. I recently opened a savings account with a bank because they advertised how they would give me $200 free if I opened an account with them. All I had to do was put in $1,000 to fund the account and I would earn $200 within the next month for free.

I read all the rules for this free money and found that I could put the money in a savings account and then as soon as I received my $200 I could pull my money back out and use it however I want. The only thing that they required was that I would keep the savings account open for six months with a regular withdrawal of the minimum of $25 from my checking account into the savings account. I saw this as a way to make $200 in 15 minutes, so I jumped on it. That comes out to $800 for one hour of work!

For me, a bank savings account is not a way that I invest my money, but a way that I park my money until I can invest it in more real estate. If you must invest your money in a savings account because it is one of the safest ways to "invest" your money, I would advise you find the bank that has the highest interest rate.

b. Certificate of Deposit

- **Risk: Extremely Low** – Extremely unlikely you will lose your money

- **Reward: Extremely Low** – Currently earn 1.010% monthly on average

- **Liquidity: Moderate** – You can take your money out at the end of the term or pay a penalty

A certificate of deposit (CD) is a timed deposit where you indicate to the bank a specific amount of time you will let them hold onto your money for a higher return than a normal savings account. The time frames for the CD vary depending on the bank, but they can be in one, five, or ten-year increments. I visit www.bankrate.com to find interest rates on local and nationwide banks for CDs and other interest-bearing accounts.

A CD is beneficial to the bank because they are given a specific amount of time that they can lend your money to someone else at a higher rate. If you withdraw it before the CDs maturity date, you will pay a penalty for pulling out early and breaking the contract that you signed with the bank. The benefit for you is that you get a slightly higher interest rate for your money than in a savings account. The liquidity is the problem though. The level is moderate because you can still pull out your money, but you will pay a penalty for doing so.

c. Money Market Accounts

- **Risk: Extremely Low** – Extremely unlikely you will lose your money

- **Reward: Extremely Low** – Currently earn 1.05% monthly on average

- **Liquidity: Extremely High** – You can take your money out very easily

A money market account is a non-financial account that pays interest based on the current interest rates in the money market. Again, I go to www.bankrate.com to find the best money market accounts they offer the best return. These do have low risk and relatively low reward, but the liquidity is fairly high. The downside with a money market is you usually need higher deposit amount than a savings account or a CD. Sometimes, the minimum would be $25,000 deposited in the account or you would incur a monthly fee.

4. Investing in the Stock Market - Dividends

- **Financial Risk: Moderate** –If the company does poorly on its earnings the stock price will go down.

- **Financial Reward: Moderate** – The stock market gains typically 8% to 10% per year.

- **Financial Liquidity: High** – You can take your money out very easily.

- **$ Requirement: Low to Very High**

- **Time Commitment: Moderate to High**

Investing in stocks, bonds, mutual funds, etc. is basically giving your money over to someone else to use. In the stock market you are buying a part of a company, which is called a share in the company. The value of that stock goes up and down as the company earns or loses money. With stocks, there are only two things you can do to make money: Hope and Wait.

You must hope and wait for the value of the shares to increase so you can then sell it at a higher price. An individual investor has no say in the company and how it is run. The board of directors and the CEO are the ones who lead the company to either make a profit or lose money.

One positive note, I can see possibly investing in stocks to buy into a company that pays dividends. Anyone can invest in a dividend paying stock which pays monthly or quarterly dividends (profits the company made above all expenses) which is a good way to have cash flow coming in. The bad thing is that you need to invest millions of dollars in order to get any sort of dividend to live off of.

If you invest in a good company and their profits continually go up, the price of the stock will go up. If you buy the stock at a low price and the company does well year after year, your shares should increase and then you have gained value. If you buy the shares at a high price and sell them at a low price you lose value. You realize your gains or losses when you sell the shares, not when you buy them. I personally do not put my money in the stock market for many reasons.

I wrote two posts on my blog called "_10 Ginormous Problems with Your 401K_" and "_7 Traps in Your IRA the Rich Do Not Fall For_". In these posts, I share how you are losing money with these "investing" plans. I personally do not "invest" my money in a 401k and an IRA.

Once I learned the problems in these plans, I pulled all my money out and invested it into rental properties. Even though I got hit with taxes, I have made that money back and much more pulling my money out and investing them in real estate.

The bottom line is that you and I cannot control any of the companies in the stock market, thus cannot control the return on the money invested. I have personally lost over $10,000 in the stock market on a few different occasions trying to learn how to invest in the market. After those losses, I realized that I do not enjoy investing in stock market and have found out that there are many better ways to invest.

Now, I will say that there are many great investors who do a great job investing in stocks. The two people that come to mind quickly for me are Warren Buffett and Jim Rogers. These two men are brilliant investors in the stock market and have earned millions of dollars from it.

Jim Rogers made so much money that he doesn't have to work anymore as he could live off the dividends that the stocks payout. Warren Buffett continues to invest in the stock market, probably because he enjoys it, and he's superb at it. Many such men and women do terrific in the stock market. I know that I am just not one of those people.

CHAPTER 16

BUSINESS MODEL OF CONTENT CREATION

"Innovation distinguishes between a leader and a follower."

- Steve Jobs

CREATING CONTENT THAT OTHERS WILL CONTINUALLY BUY

A much different way to earn passive income would be by spending your time rather than your money. The most expensive thing that you can spend in your life is not your money, but your time. Time is the only thing that you can never get back once it is spent. You can't earn any more of it and you only have a limited amount of time to spend. For this reason, working a job for a living is spending an hour of your time for a defined amount of money.

That time that you spent working for the wage you earn may have been spent making more money in a different career. Also, your time could have been spent creating passive income generating businesses that would continually pay you after that one hour that you worked.

This idea is a way to get paid a royalty for the thing that you produced and that others will sell. Think of how much money the rock band the Beatles have earned over these many years. Each time one of their songs is played they get a royalty from the company who is playing the song.

It may have taken the Beatles four or five hours to write and record the song "A Hard Day's Night" but they are still getting paid today from the royalties it generates whenever it's played.

Think about a famous author like Stephen King who has written hundreds of books and continually gets paid whenever one is sold. This is a lasting creation from the author that will continually bring in passive income from the royalties it produces. Stephen King may take one to two months to write a book, but will make millions from that one book depending on how it sells.

What about creating a blog or podcast that you can create to inform your readers and listeners of anything that might interest them? That is also a form of passive income where you spend an hour working, yet get paid continually.

With my blog, I can gather readers of my content, and I can also gather listeners from my podcast. I am also able to refer these readers and listeners to goods and services that would benefit them, and I would make a commission for referring them.

Ways to Make Money with Content Creation:

a. Create a Product: Ask the customers what they are looking for so you can create a solution for them. Create the product and sell it to customers.

b. Sponsorship: Find companies who want to market to your listeners and charge them a fee for sponsoring a podcast where you mention them in the episode.

c. Affiliates Sales: You can refer your readers and listeners to an affiliate company who give you a share of the revenue from the sales that you bring them.

d. Start a Membership/Mastermind Group: start a membership group where your customers pay a monthly membership to be a part of the group. This group would bring a benefit to the customer and help them in whatever they are currently doing.

e. Mentoring/Coaching: find others who want to do what you are currently doing and mentor/coach them in how you did it so that they can learn and do the same.

f. Public Speaking: share your content with thousands of individuals at the same time from a stage and get paid for it.

5. Blogging

- **Financial Risk: N/A**

- **Financial Reward: Low to Extremely High**

- **Financial Liquidity: N/A**

- **$ Requirement: Low to Moderate**

- **Time Commitment: Moderate**

The blogging business can be one of the best types of passive income businesses for those who have a passion that they want to share with the world. Some bloggers make over $100,000 a month in passive income from their blogs. These guys are the exception, but imagine if you could get just 1% of that each month. That would be an extra $1000 a month in your pocket that you would never have had in the first place.

The more time and effort you put into your blog, the more money you can potentially make. As you put more content into your blog, more people find your site because search engines start to promote you more as you are more relevant. If you are not putting good content up, people will not want to read your blog and that will make search engines less likely to promote you because they only want to promote relevant sites to their users.

Don't be intimidated by the idea of creating a blog. It is very easy and cheap. It just takes a bit of learning, as anything new does, and your effort to make it work. So, what should you blog about? I suggest you blog about what you are passionate about. If you chose something that is not your passion, you may give up quickly because your heart is not in it.

The key is that it doesn't matter what your passion is because there is a market for it. If your passion is turning pallets into nice functional furniture, a blog sharing how to turn pallets into nice furniture and accessories around the house would be a nice fit. Or if your passion is to collect baseball cards to buy and sell them, a blog teaching how to grade, trade, sell, and buy cards would be right up your alley.

For example, my brother has a passion for playing poker. That's right, the Texas Hold'em kind of poker. He decided he wanted to have a blog teaching people how to play poker. He started his blog, www.smartpokerstudy.com in 2015 and already has thousands of readers/listeners and is making money each month from his passion.

For you, find what your passion is and start looking for blogs that teach what you love. Learn from them how they are using their blog to see what they are doing right and wrong.

If you plan to start a blog, there are a few resources I suggest and have used, to help my blog businesses.

Web Hosting: Bluehost is a good cheap hosting service that you can get hosting for as little as $7.95 a month. Use this link to get a discount on your service down to $3.95 a month. *http://www.bluehost.com/*

Domain Name Registration:
Namecheap.com is a great place for buying domain names for as little as $7 for a one-year purchase. Go through this link to get your domain at a discount: *http://www.namecheap.com/*

WordPress Installation: Once you have these two set up and working, all you need to do is install the blogging platform WordPress onto your site for free. With these in place, you now have a fully functioning blog that will reach millions of people around the world with your content. The total cost for these components of your blog is only $10 and you are up and running with your own blog.

Extra Resources: For those of you who would like to purse blogging as a way to earn passive income check out this great online blogging course. *http://www.masterpassiveincome.com/bloggingcourse*

6. Podcasting

- **Financial Risk: N/A**
- **Financial Reward: Low to Extremely High**
- **Financial Liquidity: N/A**
- **$ Requirement: Low to Moderate**
- **Time Commitment: Moderate**

Podcasting is a medium where you make an audio recording and upload it to the internet for others to download and listen. Being a content driven passive income idea, your content is what will help you make money because listeners will want to hear what you produce for them.

Podcasts can be entertaining, educating, or even informative. Depending on the route you want to pursue, you can make a lot of money. Podcaster John Lee Dumas has made over $500,000 a month from his podcast interviewing business owners.

My brother and I have a fun podcast called _The Walking Dead Bros Podcast_. It is a fun podcast where we both talk about the most recent episode of the Walking Dead and give our two cents on the show. We have thousands of listeners and are growing every episode.

If you would like to start podcasting, there are a few things you need:

1. Computer with internet connection
2. Good microphone to speak into
3. Headphones for listening
4. Audio editing software
5. A syndicating service like lybsin.com to publish your podcast

Extra Resources: If you would like to begin earning passive income with a podcast, I encourage you to take this great online course on podcasting and learn how to get started. This will walk you through each step of the podcasting process and bring in cash flow every month. *http://www.masterpassiveincome.com/podcastcourse*

Podcast Hosting: If you would like to start podcasting, use the promo code "Dustin" and receive two months free just for signing up! Use this link: *http://www.libsyn.com*

Microphone: The microphone I use is the one of the best condenser microphones for the price. This is a great starter to intermediate microphone that will get you started podcasting without breaking the bank. You can find it here: *www.masterpassiveincome.com/condensormicrophone*

Microphone Adjustable Arm: To hold up the microphone in one place, I use this microphone arm. It attaches to the back of my desk and extends all the way to where I am positioned in front of my computer. It is the best way to hold your microphone with your hands free. *www.masterpassiveincome.com/microphonearm*

Other Equipment: You can check out my resource page for all the other podcasting equipment you will need to set your podcasting business up right. *www.masterpassiveincome.com/podcasting-equipment*

7. Build an App for Smart Phones

- **Financial Risk: N/A**

- **Financial Reward: Low to Extremely High**

- **Financial Liquidity: N/A**

- **$ Requirement: Low to High**

- **Time Commitment: Moderate to High**

The world has been going the way of mobile phones for many years now and with them come applications to run on them. These applications are called apps and millions of people use them around the world.

It used to be that only big companies with lots of money could create software programs that would run on desktop computers for everyone to use. A company needed a lot of money and many employees to create a program that will sell successfully in the market.

Now, because of cell phones, an app can be built for little to no money out of your pocket. The only thing you need is the ability/knowledge of how to code and program the app to do what you want it to do.

Most people do not know how to write software code, let alone how to build an app that would sell to millions of people. For those who are interested in developing an app, there are many programmers out there that would love to code your app for you.

I use the website *www.fiverr.com* for all my programming work. This site works like this: Someone posts their ability they would be willing to do for $5. You hire them to do what they say they will do and give them directions. Once they are done, you inspect their work and then pay them if you are satisfied.

I've spent hundreds of dollars on this website, but I have made my money back tenfold. Passive income is all about having others do the work for you and this is a great way to find someone to do that for you.

Once you have your app created, you can post it on iTunes, Google Play, Kindle, etc. for others to purchase. You no longer need to go into big box stores to sell your product. Now, there are millions of ready buyers to buy your app at the touch of a button.

Extra Resources: Here is an online app building course that you can use to get your app business off the ground. This will help you from start to finish to begin making money online with your app. *www.masterpassiveincome.com/appbuildingcourse*

8. Book and eBook Writing

- **Financial Risk: N/A**
- **Financial Reward: Low to Extremely High**
- **Financial Liquidity: N/A**
- **$ Requirement: Low to Moderate**
- **Time Commitment: Moderate**

The process of writing a book is much easier than one may think. If you graduated high school, then you have already been taught how to write a book. Book writing is truly a passive income business. You write a book one time and it sells itself over and over again.

Writing and selling a book is the easiest it has been in the history of bookmaking. With the ability to create eBooks, print-on-demand books, and online retailers who are ready to sell your books without any upfront printing costs.

There is no longer a need for a publisher to publish your book since you can now be your own publisher. All you need is a computer and an internet connection and you are up and running as a publisher/writer. My first book, "How to Quit Your Job with Rental Properties" I self-published and have for sale on many online book websites.

I know of one self-published author who makes over $40,000 a month from the sales of all his books. He does have over two dozen books for sale that he has written over a number of years. The biggest thing to understand is that in order to sell more books you need to write more books. Each successful book you write brings attention to your other books and leads to more sales.

If you are interested in book writing, here are the steps you need to follow to write a book:

1. Come up with a topic you have a passion to talk about

2. Develop three sections of your book, beginning, middle, conclusion

3. Create an outline from the three sections that helps to explain the sections

4. Create content for the outline using the outline as chapters for your book

5. Proof-read your book and make it readable

6. Hire someone on *fiverr.com* to edit/proof-read your book

7. Hire someone on *fiverr.com* to create a cover

8. Hire someone on *fiverr.com* to format your book for eBooks and paperbacks

9. Upload your finished work to online retailers

10. Market your book

11. Earn passive income while your book sells itself

Extra Resource: For those of you who would like to learn more about how to write and publish a book on Amazon and other online retailers, this online course will give you the blueprint to be successful. The course will take you step-by-step from idea to completed print book and help you gain passive income through book writing.

http://www.masterpassiveincome.com/bookwritingcourse

9. Create a Niche Website

- ■ **Financial Risk: N/A**
- ■ **Financial Reward: Low to Extremely High**
- ■ **Financial Liquidity: N/A**
- ■ **$ Requirement: Low to Moderate**
- ■ **Time Commitment: Moderate**

Creating a niche website is just like creating a blog but is a bit more hands-off. The goal of a blog is to create a following of people so they listen to what you have to say and eventually pay you to teach them more.

The goal of a niche website is to reach as many different people one time. An example would be a product that has just hit the market and people want to know how to use it, where to buy it, and what others are saying about it.

Let's say you want to create a niche site on the best camping and survival knives on the market right now. This would be perfect for a niche site because there is a limited amount of information you would need to create to help your readers find the knife they want and purchase the knife through an affiliate link on an online store where you make money from the sale.

Here are some keys to a good niche website:

1. Very specific in content and audience

2. Detailed information on all the aspects of the product, service, or other

3. Compare the product/service with others to help your readers understand what is the best item for them to purchase

4. Link to the online stores for the reader to purchase the product through your affiliate link

5. Make the site very eye catching with visuals, videos, write-ups, etc.

With these keys, a niche website can do very well reaching many people and making good money. There is a lot of time involved with creating the content for the site but it will all pay off as people start buying through your site.

Extra Resource: Much like building a blog website, a niche site will allow you to make passive income through affiliate sales. The key difference is the content you will be promoting. Get started learning how the steps to a profitable web niche course today with the online course how to build a niche website: *www.masterpassiveincome.com/websitenichecourse*

10. Create YouTube Videos

■ **Financial Risk: N/A**

■ **Financial Reward: Low to Extremely High**

■ **Financial Liquidity: N/A**

■ $ **Requirement: Low to Moderate**

■ **Time Commitment: Moderate**

Creating YouTube videos is similar to all other content creation ideas in that your content is what people desire. The only difference is the medium in which you deliver it. This medium is through videos as opposed to written text or audible voice.

Creating this can be the scariest of all the passive income ideas because you are putting yourself behind the camera for the entire world to see. Once you get past those fears, the passive income business creating videos can be a very lucrative business.

Like all other content business, the more people that view your product, the more you get paid. If you create a viral video that millions of viewers watch, you can make lots of money in advertising and endorsements.

You are creating your own "channel" as another TV channel. The only difference is the cost to make these videos is nothing compared to big budget companies who spend lots of money making TV shows.

So, what does it take to make money on YouTube and other video sites? The only thing you need is a video camera (which most people already have on their phone) and start recording. Now you must have great content that others would want to watch.

Like a blog or podcast, take what you are passionate about and make videos for everyone to consume. The more passion you have for something the more likely you will be successful with the business.

Quick Tip: You can use the camera on your computer. Usually it is a webcam but it can be used to record your videos. Another great tool is your smart phone that already has a HD quality camera. I have made many videos for my business with my phone. The quality is great and I already had the phone!

11. Online Course Creation

- **Financial Risk: N/A**

- **Financial Reward: Low to Extremely High**

- **Financial Liquidity: N/A**

- **$ Requirement: Low**

- **Time Commitment: Moderate**

Much like writing a book, placing a for sale sign on it and waiting for people to buy it, an online course is a truly passive income at its best. Once you create the course, you don't have to do any more work on it because the content is ready for a new customer to access it and pay you for your knowledge.

In creating a course, think of how you would create a non-fiction book that teaches a topic you have passion for. The only difference is how you deliver that content to your customers.

With online courses, your medium is both print and video. Most people enjoy learning by video where the instructor is teaching the topic as almost a one-on-one setting. With you as the teacher, it is just you in front of the camera teaching the content to the student.

If you are interested in creating an online course, here are the general steps you need to follow:

1. Come up with a topic you have passion for

2. Develop three to six sections of your course

3. Create an outline from the three sections that helps to explain the sections

4. Create videos for the outline using the outline as sections of your course

5. Edit and review your videos

6. Upload your finish work to an online course site, or your own WordPress site

7. Market your online course

If you have more interest in learning about on-line courses, check out this online course that will help you to put on your own online course. *http://www.masterpassiveincome.com/onlinecourse*

12. Teaching Webinars

■ **Financial Risk: N/A**

■ **Financial Reward: Low to Extremely High**

■ **Financial Liquidity: N/A**

■ **$ Requirement: Low**

■ **Time Commitment: Moderate**

Webinars are short seminars that are online for others to watch and learn what you are teaching them. Regarding content, your content is a condensed version of an online course.

In an online course, you itemize each step of the training from A to Z; the webinar gives the main points in a 1 to 2-hour session. Just like how Tony Robins sells his seminars to teach people from a stage for an hour or two, you will be doing the same thing.

The main difference is that the webinar is online and is done through webinar companies that allow you to connect with your users. Usually, webinars are ways to sell more products that you offer like your online course.

Sky Matsuhashi sells his webinar courses for $50 each participant on different aspects of playing poker. Others use their webinar to sell their books, other people's online courses, and to reach more people for their products.

Webinars are a great way to engage with your audience like no other medium. It is a direct connection with them where you can interact in a group setting and get to know them better.

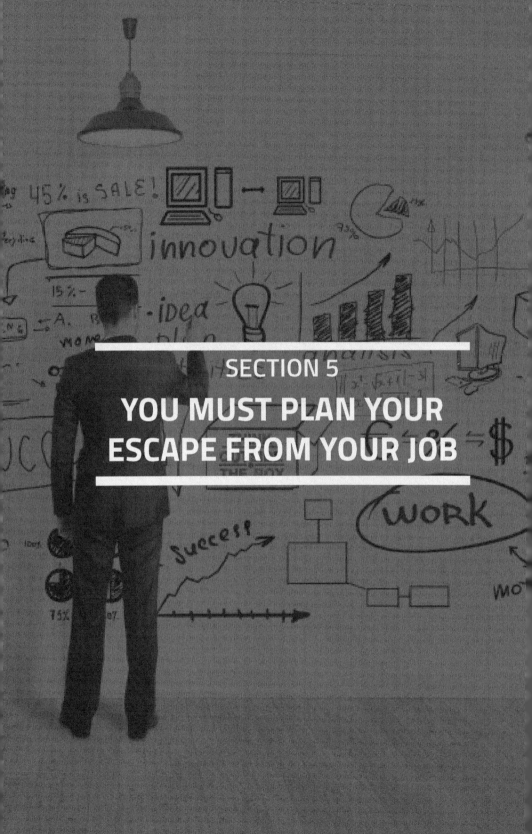

YOU MUST PLAN YOUR ESCAPE FROM YOUR JOB

CHAPTER 17

THE BLUEPRINT TO PLAN AN ESCAPE FROM YOUR JOB

"The ones who are crazy enough to think they can change the world, are the ones who do."

- Anonymous

So, how do you plan your escape from your job? Is there some sort of formula, step by step direction, or a road map that will get you there? I believe that it can be all of the above.

I have already blazed the trail in making passive income with my rental properties so that I can quit my job.

Quitting your job and living off your passive income is a very scary thing to do. It is not easy to do the things we are scared to do. The passive income ideas and strategies I have increase my passive income above and beyond my earned income so I can now quit my job.

In this section are the things to think through to enable you quit your job in a responsible way.

INCOME

How much income do you need to survive? How are you going to pay your rent or mortgage, food bills, gas, insurance, etc. if you do not have any income? Let's say that you do quit your job, how are you going to make money? How much money will you need to live on? Your earned income is now gone so you need to develop your passive income so money will keep coming in each month.

A big question that you have hopefully already answered for yourself is how you will make your income now that you have quit your job. Remember that when you are working a job, you are earning what is called earned income. You want to get away from earned income and work hard to gain passive income.

Passive income is when you work one time and continually be paid for the work you did. For example, it takes me about three hours to purchase a rental property and I get paid every single month because of the rent I charge for someone to live in my property. There's no way to actually quantify the hourly wage I am making from those three hours I worked buying the house because the income continually grows each month.

The only time I would be able to calculate my hourly wage is if I sell the property and stop making money from the rents.

Another example is my best selling book _"How to Quit Your Job with Rental Properties: A_

Step-by-Step Guide to Unlocking Passive In-
come Investing In Real Estate" that I wrote and
sell on my website and other online retailers.

I believe it took me close to 80 hours to write, edit,
produce, and publish the book, but each time the
book sells, I make money. I did all the work up front,
creating the book and now the book is paying me
continually and helping thousands of people with
their goal to quit their job with passive income.

As you saw in the chapter on finding your
investment vehicle, what you invest your time and
money in is vital to quitting your job with passive
income. I encourage you to find what excites you
and dive right in. Start the passive income process
today because in 5-10 years, you could possibly be
ready to quit your job!

LIVING EXPENSES

In today's world, just about everyone needs money to
survive. Unless you're living on a homestead in Alaska,
money is an important part of living. If you are like the
rest of us, you need to have a regular monthly income
in order to live. This is where passive income fills the
void of not having a steady paycheck. With the passive income though, you need to figure out how much
income you need each month in order to live your life.

To find out how much income you need each month in passive cash flow, you need to calculate all of your expenses and total them up. Be sure to add everything that takes money out of your pocket each month. Rent, cell phone bill, food, utilities, Internet, cable TV, insurance, car payment, student loan payment, credit card payment, etc. Make sure you get everything down on paper so you know what you are spending each month to cover your expenses.

After you have all these items written down, add them all up to get your total expenses for the month. Go to my website and download and fill out the quick _budget worksheet (http://www.masterpassiveincome. com/quickbudget)_ to find your total living expenses. Total all your expenses up and that is your total living expenses you need to cover with your passive income if you are to quit your job.

I personally suggest adding another 20% to your living expenses so you can save for future investment. If you currently have expenses that are $3000 a month you need to get enough passive income that covers $3000 plus another 20% on top of that equaling $3600 a month in income. You should be saving and the extra $600 a month and only spending it on investments that bring you more money into your pocket.

SHORTEN THE TIME-LINE TO QUIT YOUR JOB

Another way to accelerate your ability to quit your job would be to reduce your expenses along with increasing your passive income. If you are spending the same $3,000 a month, try cutting your expenses by 30% to accelerate your ability to quit your job.

There are many ways to reduce your expenses. What you need to do is be objective when you look at your expenses. Look at what your money goes to each month and ask yourself, "Do I really need to be spending my money on this?"

It could be cutting out cable television, super high-speed Internet, over expensive cell phone and plans, eating out less, and many other simple ways to reduce your expenses. Hopefully, you can find some things you can cut out of your monthly expenses.

You must know how much it costs for you to pay for the necessities of life. And no, a latte at Starbucks is not a necessity. Wait to buy those when you have already quit your job and have enough money to splurge on items like this.

Both increasing your passive income and decreasing your expenses will get you on the fast track to quitting your job.

SAVINGS

No matter how much money you bring in with passive income, the wise thing to do is always to have a savings and an emergency fund. Your savings is where you store all your money that you are going to invest into passive income producing properties or other ideas that will generate cash flow each month.

The emergency fund is something that you do not use to spend on luxury items or investing or anything else. It is there just for emergencies to help you out of a tough spots and handle the ebb and flow of your passive income.

Since your income is not constant as a salary or an hourly wage, some months are better than others, and some months can be pretty bad. Just like a salesman who earns his living from a commission, some months have better sales than others. You need to be ready for the bad months by saving during the good months.

Speaking of bad months, I went off track with my spending in year eight of my 10-year plan and spent way too much money. Usually, I have anywhere from $6,000-$8,000 coming in each month and I spent as it had always come in. There was a three-month stretch where through evictions, tenants moving out, late rents, etc. I had a fraction of my regular income coming in.

So instead of a $6,000 check I got a $200 check one month, a $400 check the next month, then a $17 check the following month. These were some terrible months for me and I learned a big lesson because it took me off my path and set me back at least 6 to 8 months behind schedule.

I had a small amount saved in my interest-bearing account, maybe two months' worth of expenses, but I ran through that pretty quick. With my horrible spending habits and my passive income bringing in a fraction of the total income as it usually did, I had to go into my savings in order to pay for things that I normally would have no concern about. After that storm, I changed everything.

I cut my expenses and spending dramatically and have been working hard to make my passive income as regular and consistent as possible. Be it through evicting bad tenants, lowering rents by 10% to keep people in the unit, to getting section eight tenants in my properties.

From that point forward I made it my goal not to spend money. I learnt my lesson and after that, I started taking pride in not spending any money other than absolute necessities. If something broke, I fixed it myself or did without it.

If we would normally eat out, I decided that we were to cut how much we were spending on food in half and made Top Ramen or PB & jelly sandwiches. Now I know that life is short and you want to spend your money the way you want, buying lattes, going out to lunch every day, etc. but my opinion is that you save that life to when you can afford it through your passive income and you have already quit your job.

I suggest having around three to six months saved in an interest-bearing account. The account I use is through *www.CapitalOne.com*. I find they have the highest interest rate for savings and checking accounts. I have received as much as 1.025% per month interest on my checking account with Capital One. Since most savings accounts only give you .02% per year, this Capital One is AMAZING! Right now, if you *go through this link (http://www.masterpassiveincome.com/capitalone)*, you will get $25 just for signing up!

So, how much money will you need in an emergency fund for those unexpected expenses? Take your monthly expenses, not including the 20% increase for investing; multiply it by three to get the minimum amount you need saved in your Capital One account to be safe for life's ups and downs. Now multiply your expenses by six to get your maximum amount you need saved. You can obviously go over this amount but it would be better to invest that money and have it make you even more money.

Now that you have your target amount for your emergency fund, chip away at it with each paycheck and passive income you earn. I personally save $1,000 each month from my paycheck and put it towards my emergency fund. It is not easy, but you can do it if you put your mind to it.

HEALTH INSURANCE FOR YOU
AND YOUR FAMILY

Health insurance for you and your family can be almost a deal breaker for most people desiring to quit their job. I have seen many people keep working well beyond retirement because their employer is paying the majority of their health insurance and they believe they can't afford to pay for it on their own.

How Sad is That?

Someone works their entire life and is forced into working even longer just to pay for their health insurance. Now that they are older and have their health deteriorating, they cannot retire/quit because they do not have enough money to pay for health insurance. That does not sound very appealing to me.

The best way to approach your health insurance is to look at it like it is a commodity. It's something that you can shop around for and get better prices with other companies. Just because your employer pays for a portion of your health insurance, you shouldn't automatically go with that insurance. The best time to plan for your health insurance is when you don't actually need it.

If you currently have a job where you already have health insurance, work towards getting off your employer based health insurance and find something that you can afford that will take care of your needs.

It may very well be that you are personally overpaying for your insurance that you can get from another company that you pay out of your pocket.

The last job I ever had offered health insurance as a benefit of being employed there. The costs for my entire family for their health care were $1200 a month! That is a lot of money each month for anyone to be paying for health insurance. Adding insult to injury (pun intended) we rarely went to the doctor since we were a young healthy family that only went to the doctor about once a year.

I knew we didn't need to pay that much for health insurance. So, I started looking for health insurance outside of my job to compare the type of coverage and the costs associated with them.

I believed that I could at least get my health insurance costs cut in half by finding my own insurance. I got different quotes from different insurance companies and also looked to other types of health coverage. After going through all the big names in the business to find which was good and had much better rates for me, I found a company that fits my family's needs. I saved over $8000 a year in premium payments and put that in my savings instead of paying it to the insurance company.

SPENDING HABITS

I have already shared my mistake in my spending habits and how spending too much money took me down the wrong path and cost me eight months to get back on the path to quitting my job. What about you? Do you spend all that you earn or even more? Are you going into debt with all the spending you do? Without controlling your spending, you will surely run out of money fast.

My wife and I were raised not to have consumer debt. Consumer debt is where you buy liabilities that do not bring on any money into your pocket. I was always taught to pay off my credit card balance every single month so I did not incur any interest. One time I did not pay the full balance, and I got hit with an interest charge. Seeing that extra charge just for borrowing their money made me realize that I hate paying interest on things that are not making me any money.

Because we were both raised not to have any consumer debt, we started off on the right foot and did not have to dig out of a hole that we created with extra debt saddled on us. Maybe you may have consumer debt that is eating away at your cash every month. You could be starting with $10,000, $30,000, or even $50,000 or more in consumer debt. This is something that you need to attack viciously to start down the path of passive income.

There are two things here that we need to be concerned about. The first one is the amount of debt that you currently have, and the other is how much more debt you accumulate each month with your spending. Are you spending more than you bring in?

The way to figure out if you are going into debt is to take your income minus your expenses. If you have greater expenses than your income, then you are going into debt every month.

The first step is to stop spending more than you make in so you don't continue going into debt. Everyone has the ability to cut something out of their expenses and it's your job to now take a hatchet (metaphorically) and hack away at your expenses until you get under your income and stop going into debt. It could be something as simple as bring a sack lunch to work every day instead of going out to eat.

It could be something as drastic as selling the $30,000 car that you have a loan on and are making a monthly payment of $600. Whatever it is in your expenses, be brutal and go after the expenses that are eating you alive. Just think about how much money you are wasting on interest each month because you are over spending.

Now that you've stopped overspending, you can start attacking the debt that you currently have accumulated.

Let me give you an example.

If you have three credit cards and three other loans that all have a balance on them, I suggest you attack the card that has the least amount of total debt on it. The reason why I suggest doing this is because you have the ability to get a quick win under your belt by getting rid of this one credit card faster than all the others.

The other reason is that once this credit card payment is gone, you are now able to take the payment that you had been paying on it and now apply that amount to the next lowest balance card. Each time you pay off a card, you combine that money to your payment on the next card you are trying to pay off. You will be able to get rid of this card even faster because you now have more money to put towards the principal balance.

What you need to remember is that your spending habits will help or hurt you on your way to financial freedom. The more you spend the less money you have to invest. The less you spend, the more you have to invest.

FUTURE INVESTMENT

Believe me; I know that it's hard to gain enough passive income just to replace your earned income, let alone any extra income for investing. Even though it's hard to do, you want to make sure that you can continually grow your passive income by having enough cash on hand to invest.

As I stated earlier, I believe that a real goal would be to have surpassed your earned income with your passive income by 20%. So, whatever your earned income is, you want your passive income to be 120% of that total.

If you're currently earning $3,000 a month, your goal should be $3,600 a month in passive income. With that extra $600, you can invest it back into other income producing assets that will bring in more money. So if you save $600 for one entire year you have another $7,200 to invest for your future. After two years that's $14,400 that you can invest into the future.

Imagine This With Me

Your passive income is like a snowball that you create with your hands. It looks rather small in your hands, but once you set it in motion by rolling a down a snow-covered hill, it will get bigger and bigger and roll faster and faster as it goes down the hill. So, think of your passive income like a snowball. Your initial investment of $7,200 could be that small snowball in your hands. You use that $7,200 to purchase one rental property that brings in an extra $300 a month which would be an extra $3,600 on top of the $7,200 you earn in the second year.

That is a total of $10,800 in the second year that you can invest. Now you take that $10,800 and you buy another rental property that brings in another $300 each month in passive income. That would be another $3,600 a year that you can use to invest in assets that bring you money every month. Now your total is $14,400 each year that you can invest.

With this money, you can purchase rental properties and bring in $600 more each month with these new properties. That would be another $7,200 on top of the $14,400 for a total passive income of $21,600 each year!

How amazing would that be if you continue this process for five, 10, or even 15 years? That snowball that started in your hands grew to a massive passive income producing gargantuan snowball.

If you follow this plan, you will continually grow your income over and over and make money hand over fist with your passive income. And remember, you are not doing any work because this is all passive income.

SECTION 6
THE FINISH

CHAPTER 18

GET STARTED NOW!

*"What's the point of being alive
if you don't at least try to do
something remarkable."*

– Anonymous

There's no point learning and refusing to act on what has been learned. It doesn't matter if you learned all the principles from the world most successful men in history. If you do not deliberately act on them, nothing will happen. You have learned a lot about passive income being the way of the rich.

While the poor or average get to work and earn by the hour, the rich work once and earn repeatedly. Investing in passive income is the best way to secure your future financially and for you to live a relatively easy and good life.

If you desire to earn passive income, you need to find the investment vehicle that will bring in the income while not getting paid for an hour that you work. I suggest you find something that you are passionate about and figure out a way to make money from it.

Learn as much as you can about the investment vehicle you decide to go with and continually learn about how you can do it better. You should never stop learning but you should only learn the things that will benefit you in the endeavor that you are seeking.

I constantly learn about online businesses and real estate investing so I can continually develop those two aspects of my life. No matter what you choose to go after, do it 100% and never give up.

Persistence is the key to the game of passive income and as you build it, it will build upon itself. The more content I create on my blog the better it gets, and the more rental properties I purchase the more money I make to purchase more rental properties.

Don't try to make money fast, try to make money wisely.

CLOSING CHALLENGE

MY CHALLANGE TO YOU
TO QUIT IN 10 YEARS

*"I find that the harder I work,
the more luck I seem to have."*

- Thomas Jefferson

Thank you very much for allowing me the opportunity to share with you the way to make passive income and change your life. I hope you have my kind of success in your businesses and in life. If you push hard and commit to passive income, you too will quit your job and live the life of your dreams.

Make your plan and then live your plan. If at first you don't succeed, try, try again. I have had countless more successes in my life but I have learned more from my failures than from my successes. Don't be afraid to fail. Failure will only help you learn and become wiser still. Whatever doesn't kill you makes you stronger.

Take this challenge I took myself all those years ago. I challenge you to quit your job in 10 years or earlier with passive income. It took me 9 years to beat my own challenge and I hope you will do the same. Work as hard as you can for passive income and you too will quit your job because you have enough money coming in to cover all your expenses.

Set a date for 10 years from today. Tell yourself that you will work as hard as you can to make enough passive income to quit your job. Remind yourself every day of this challenge. Wake up each morning with as if it is the only day that matters. Before you know it, 10 years will have gone by and you will have enough passive income to quit your J.O.B.

Now get out there and start making passive income today!

RESOURCES TO START YOUR PASSIVE INCOME BUSINESS

For all the resources mentioned in this book, you can access a complete list online here:
http://www.masterpassiveincome.com/resources

Real Estate Rental Property Investing

Book: "How to Quit Your Job with Rental Properties: A Step-by-Step Guide to Investing in Real Estate and Passive Income"

http://www.masterpassiveincome.com/thebook/

Freelancers to Help Build Your Business:

http://www.fiverr.com

Blogging

Web Hosting:
http://www.bluehost.com

Domain Name Registration:
http://www.namecheap.com/

WordPress Installation:
http://www.wordpress.org

Online Course:
http://www.masterpassiveincome.com/bloggingcourse

Podcasting

Online Podcasting Course:
http://www.masterpassiveincome.com/podcastcourse

Podcast Hosting: *www.libsyn.com* promo code "Dustin" for 2 free months.

Other Equipment: *http://www.masterpassiveincome. com/podcasting-equipment*

Build an App for Smart Phones

App Building Courset: *http://www.masterpassiveincome. com/appbuildingcourse*

Book and eBook Writing

Book Writing Course: *http://www.masterpassiveincome. com/bookwritingcourse*

Create a Niche Website

Niche Website Course: *http://www.masterpassiveincome. com/websitenichecourse*

Online Course Creation

Online Course Course: *www.masterpassiveincome. com/onlinecourse*

WILL YOU HELP OTHERS QUIT THEIR JOBS WITH PASSIVE INCOME?

I f you enjoyed How to Quit Your Job with Passive Income, would you mind taking a minute to write a review on Amazon? Even a short review helps, and it'd mean a lot to me. The more positive reviews this book has, the more Amazon will help others see it and hopefully read it.

Please go to Amazon.com or the link below to give an honest review:
www.masterpassiveincome.com/HTQYJPassiveIncomeReview

If someone you care about is struggling with their job or income, please send him or her a copy of this book. Whether you gift it to them on Amazon or email a copy of the PDF makes no difference to me.

Finally, if you'd like to get free bonus materials from this book and receive updates on my future projects, you can sign up for the Master Passive Income newsletter at *www.MasterPassiveIncome.com*

You can also follow me and Master Passive Income on Twitter and Facebook.
Facebook: *http://www.facebook.com/masterpassiveinc/*

Twitter: *http://www.twitter.com/mpidustinheiner*

Let's quit our jobs together!

Don't Forget the Free Cheat Sheet Offer!

Free Cheat Sheet for this book!

DOWNLOAD THE CHEAT SHEET NOW!

"HOW TO QUIT YOUR JOB WITH PASSIVE INCOME"

FOR FREE!

Just to say thank you for buying this book, we'd like to give you the Cheat Sheet for "How to Quit Your Job with Passive Income"

100% FREE

DOWNLOAD FREE INSTANTLY HERE

http://www.masterpassiveincome.com/Passive-Income-Free-Offer

ABOUT THE AUTHOR

Since making the decision to be independent and quit his job, Dustin took just 9 years to accomplish his goal because of his passive income businesses.

As a businessman and entrepreneur, he has learned what it takes to build a thriving business that brings in monthly cash flow every month. As a life-long learner with a desire to build bigger and better businesses, he continues to grow his wealth and independence from ever working for someone again.

In 2006, Dustin married the love of his life and were married in Phoenix Arizona. Their struggles, trials, successes, and love strengthened their marriage and brought them closer together. They both work together on their passive income businesses and they continue to be successfully married with their four children.

Dustin has a passion and a gift of teaching the things he is passionate about. He enjoys helping others achieve success in all areas of life and encourages them to push through their limiting beliefs that are holding them back. Countless others have learned how to use passive income to bring in monthly cash flow with his help.

Dustin has already quit his job and lives the dream every day. He is the founder of Master Passive Income, a company dedicated to helping people achieve financial freedom with passive income.

Dustin and his lovely wife Melissa have four children and are blessed by the Lord to be saved by His grace.

OTHER BOOKS WRITTEN BY DUSTIN HEINER

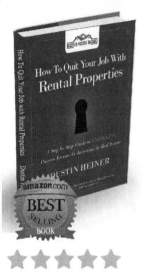

How to Quit Your Job with Rental Properties

A Step-by-Step guide to Passive Income
by Investing in Real Estate

The problem that affects almost everyone today is being stuck in a career they hate. People are conditioned to work their lives away for someone else and only get paid for the hour they work. How would you like to quit your job today because you have enough passive income to live off of?

This book contains step-by-step training to help you acquire rental properties to allow you to quit your job and be financially free so you will never have to work again. Designed for the newbie or seasoned pro, anyone will learn how they can earn passive income from rental properties and quit their job.

Follow the proven path to financial freedom that many have already successfully navigated.

Lasting Marriage

Discovering God's Meaning and
Purpose for Your Relationship

Is your marriage living the true meaning and purpose of marriage? Do you want your marriage to last through all that life throws at you? Would you like to see your marriage benefit from having more love, joy, and intimacy?

Lasting Marriage is an encouraging and insightful book that will help your marriage grow and strengthen in love and service to each other. You will learn how your marriage can become one of those success stories you hear about. You will be more in love with your spouse at your 50th wedding anniversary than on your wedding day. By knowing and applying God's meaning and purpose of marriage into your relationship, you will have a lasting marriage.

Made in the USA
Columbia, SC
28 March 2018